JOHNS HOPKINS

Portrait
of
a
University

by John C. Schmidt

1986
The Johns Hopkins University
Baltimore, Maryland

Published by the Office of University Publications
The Johns Hopkins University

Library of Congress catalog card number 86-61679

CONTENTS

PREFACE

This history of The Johns Hopkins University is an out-growth of two earlier treatments of the subject: *Johns Hopkins: Portrait of a University* and *Johns Hopkins: Centennial Portrait of a University* by Robert P. Sharkey, published in 1961 and 1975, respectively. Their purpose—and that of this revised and updated edition—is to present a concise look at the impact Johns Hopkins has made upon higher education in America over the years and to describe some of the unique ways in which the University contributes to international scholarship and science today.

No single volume can more than skim the surface of such a vast landscape. Thus we are grateful for the existence of such scholarly treatments of the University's history as those of John C. French, Hugh Hawkins, and Thomas B. Turner, among others, as well as for numerous historical articles in the *Johns Hopkins Magazine* and other shorter treatments. What this volume attempts to provide is an overview. For readers desiring deeper investigation of specific subjects, a wealth of additional material is available.

This author is the beneficiary of Dr. Sharkey's work covering the years up to the University's centennial in 1976. In the course of preparations for that event—and for two major fund-raising campaigns in recent years—some interesting new information was brought to light, and much analytical thought was devoted to the place of Johns Hopkins in the world of ideas. The text from the earlier volumes has been revised and augmented accordingly. New material brings the University's history up to the end of 1985.

Special gratitude is owed to Vice President and Secretary of the University Ross Jones—a 1953 alumnus who has served the University since the first administration of Milton Eisenhower—for his constant encouragement and support of this project. Thanks are also in order to those who assisted the author in assembling information and developing perspectives on events of enormous complexity. They include President Steven Muller, Deans George W. Fisher, Stanley C. Gabor, Carol J. Gray, Donald A. Henderson, George R. Packard, Richard S. Ross, and V. David VandeLinde; Peabody director

Robert Pierce; and William Buchanan, Susan Crowley, Elaine Freeman, and Anne Garside of the public affairs staffs. The careful reading of the text by University Archivist Julia Morgan is greatly appreciated, as is the work of Leslye Sugar and the staff of the Office of University Publications for their skills in designing and producing this volume.

John C. Schmidt

Baltimore, Maryland, January 1986

In the beginning there was Gilman

The Johns Hopkins University came into being in Baltimore in the last quarter of the 19th century. Its founding in that place and at that time brought together substantial means that were at hand and a moment that was ripe to do something extraordinary in American education. The means was an unfettered $7 million bequest from a Quaker merchant who had made his fortune in Baltimore and who gave the institution its name as well as its financial foundation. The moment had grown out of the Industrial Revolution, which had shown—particularly in Europe—that there was to be a high degree of intimacy between national progress and higher learning.

In England, Lord Kelvin, in addition to his studies of the fundamental properties of electricity, was deeply involved in the telegraph industry. In Germany, the research and teaching of such outstanding scientists as Justus von Liebig greatly stimulated a burgeoning chemical empire. The fact that major advances in these and other areas of industry were growing out of theoretical studies in universities had led to an acceptance among Europe's technologically advanced nations of the need for a higher research function in society.

1

'… the graduate school of Harvard University, started feebly in 1870… did not thrive until the example of Johns Hopkins forced our faculty to put their strength into the development of our instruction for graduates.'

Charles W. Eliot

This awareness had not yet spread across the Atlantic when Johns Hopkins died in 1873. Higher learning had failed to find a place in the social and physical order of the United States, and the realm of theoretical science, if not totally rejected, was at best regarded with indifference. Established colleges as well as institutions that called themselves universities had been unable to implement advanced study

Johns Hopkins, a prosperous Baltimore merchant, in 1867 incorporated the University and Hospital that were to bear his name. Upon his death six years later, he left $7 million to carry out his wishes. Hopkins wisely left the implementation of his legacy to an open-minded group of trustees, who sought advice from the leading educational thinkers of the day.

and graduate research of the order that was clearly becoming an essential ingredient of the nation's economic and intellectual life.

Because it was able to build from the ground up and was given unprecedented freedom to develop academically, The Johns Hopkins University was able to overcome the inertia of indifference and implement some of the interesting new ideas from the Continent that were to shape the future structure of American society. Thus, the first great contribution of the institution established through Hopkins' bequest was the leadership role which the University played in the professionalization of knowledge in this country. It seems almost certain that the modern concept of the university would have evolved eventually in the United States if the institution bearing the name of Johns Hopkins had never existed. It is nonetheless true that Hopkins was the pioneer university in America and that it set the pace and established the standards for a host of institutions which followed. Harvard President Charles W. Eliot declared in 1902 that "the graduate school of Harvard University, started feebly in 1870 ... did not thrive until the example of Johns Hopkins forced our faculty to put their strength into the development of our instruction for graduates. And what was true of Harvard was true of every other university in the land which aspired to create an advanced school of arts and sciences."

* * *

Born in 1795 on his father's tobacco plantation in southern Maryland, Johns Hopkins (he was named for his great-grandmother, Margaret Johns) left home at the age of 17 to work for his uncle, a wholesale grocery and commission merchant in Baltimore. By the time he was 24, the young man had established a mercantile house of his own, laying a foundation for future prosperity and acquiring a reputation for unusual intelligence and business acumen. Foreseeing the vital importance of transportation from the port of Baltimore to the nation's interior, he was a dynamic force in developing the nation's first major railroad, the Baltimore & Ohio. He invested heavily in its stock, and became a director in 1847 and chairman of the finance committee in 1855. On several occasions, he used his immense private holdings to bolster the railroad's credit.

Hopkins never married, a fact that no doubt influenced his thinking in his later years when he contemplated the disposition of his accumulated wealth. Exactly how he arrived at his ultimate decision is not known; however, he had become a friend of another man of wealth with great philanthropic interests in Baltimore, George Peabody, who had founded the Peabody Institute in 1857. In any event, on August 24, 1867, 12 citizens of Baltimore formed at Hopkins' request a corporation known as The Johns Hopkins University for "the promotion of education in the State of Maryland." Twelve trustees were named, four of whom were related to Hopkins. By a similar act, The Johns Hopkins Hospital was incorporated, also with 12 trustees, all but two of whom were University trustees.

* * *

Johns Hopkins died on Christmas Eve in 1873. In his will, he left the bulk of his fortune of more than $7 million—an enormous sum in the economy of the day—to be divided equally between the University and Hospital that came to bear his name. It was the greatest single philanthropic bequest in the country's history to that date.

The benefactor was quite specific in outlining his designs for the Hospital, and one desire which he made clear proved to be of enormous significance. In a letter to the trustees written in 1873, Hopkins asserted his "wish and purpose that the institution should ultimately form a part of the medical school of that university for which I have made ample provision in my will." There is little evidence as to whether or not the founder truly understood the revolutionary nature of his desire; however, in that letter he did nothing less than usher in a new era in which a hospital would bring medical science to the bedside and a medical school would emphasize the importance of research and clinical experience.

As to the University, Hopkins was specific only to the extent that trustees were forbidden to use the principal of the bequest for buildings or current expenses; they were directed to provide certain free scholarships; and they were advised to hold and administer wisely the vast portfolio of Baltimore & Ohio Railroad stock that was the heart of the bequest. The founder displayed great wisdom in the case of the University by leaving its implementation to a carefully selected board of trustees. These were not professional educators but—like Hopkins himself—men of affairs: lawyers, merchants, bankers. They possessed a broad outlook, a lack of prejudice in educational matters, and a willingness to give weight to the best available expert advice.

From today's perspective, the judgment of the first trustees seems remarkable. Before making major decisions on the form that the new University should take, they conferred with such distinguished educators as Harvard's President Eliot, Cornell's Andrew D. White, and Michigan's James B. Angell. The board also collected many publications on higher education, further evidence that it attempted to reach decisions based on the best available knowledge. What they learned was that educators of the day felt no need for another college like the 400 that already existed in the United States. There was, however, a nearly unanimous desire for what President Angell described as "a great graduate university" that would strike out boldly toward new frontiers of knowledge. There was also general unanimity as to the one person in the country who was competent to direct such an enterprise—Daniel Coit Gilman, then president of the University of California.

5

* * *

Gilman possessed a cultured and creative mind and a firmness of purpose combined with a vision unmatched in the history of American higher education. An alumnus of Yale, he had studied in Berlin where he caught the spirit of the new German university movement and came to understand the impending importance of research. He returned to New Haven and was instrumental in establishing the research-oriented Yale Scientific School, later Sheffield. In 1872, he accepted the presidency of the University of California, which, despite its name, was an alliance of collegiate and trade schools.

At the invitation of the trustees, Gilman came to Baltimore in December 1874. In the dialogue that ensued, he explained his matured vision of an American research university which would promote creative thought and scholarship at the highest levels. The trustees heartily concurred and elected him as the new University's first president.

Gilman was authorized to travel extensively to obtain the best available counsel in designing the institution. The search led him back to Europe in the summer of 1875, where he

Daniel Coit Gilman, an American educator who had studied at Yale and in Europe before being chosen in 1875 as first president of Johns Hopkins, cast the new institution in the mold of the European research-oriented university. Johns Hopkins thus became the first American institution to stress advanced study—the first true university in the modern sense in the United States.

conferred with distinguished figures in the arts and sciences both in England and on the Continent. When he returned, Gilman was even more determined to create a new institution comparable to the greatest universities in Europe, yet distinctly American in its essential nature.

The president placed little emphasis on the physical requirements of the institution; rather, he believed in the crucial importance of attracting a faculty of great ability, paying them adequately, surrounding them with students of promise, and providing them with freedom to pursue research. To his enduring credit, Gilman's vision extended beyond the obvious fields of science and engineering as bulwarks of his new university, and encompassed the humanities as well. His first faculty consisted of five eminent scholars: Basil L. Gildersleeve in Greek; H. Newell Martin, biology; Ira Remsen, chemistry; Henry A. Rowland, physics; and J.J. Sylvester, mathematics. Because Gilman had been persuaded that the University should include undergraduate instruction as well as graduate work, he also hired Charles D. Morris as collegiate professor of Greek and Latin. Gilman's wisdom in these choices was amply demonstrated in the years that followed, as each of his appointees achieved individual distinction in the world of learning.

7

Concurrent with Gilman's insistence on faculty excellence was his recruitment of serious and highly capable students and his revolutionary concept of supporting outstanding scholars with cash stipends. Each of the University's original 20 fellows was awarded $500 a year. Hopkins historian John C. French wrote: "Probably no expenditure of $10,000 in American education has ever had so large and enduring a return from the investment." The first group of graduate fellows who enrolled in the fall of 1876 included Herbert Baxter Adams in history; Henry Carter Adams, political science; W.K. Brooks, biology; Thomas Craig, mathematics; C.R. Lanman, Sanskrit; Harmon Morse, chemistry; and Josiah Royce, philosophy. Among this group were the first of scores of Hopkins-trained scholars who moved on to colonize universities throughout the country during the next quarter-century. Others took up important government science posts and one, Walter Hines Page, later became ambassador to England.

The influence of Johns Hopkins University in its early years can scarcely be overstated. In a few unpretentious buildings on North Howard Street in downtown Baltimore, a succession of some of the most eminent scholars of the time continued to gather as faculty or students. In his concise but encompassing academic history of Johns Hopkins, *The Pioneer Century: 1876-1976,* Richard Macksey, professor in the Humanities Center, wrote:

"The original faculty was soon augmented by some newcomers who were to leave their impress on the development of the University: the philosophers G.S. Morris and Charles Sanders Peirce, the latter a polymath whose work in the logic of relations, the philosophy of mathematics and scientific method, semiotics, and pragmatism was to establish his claim as the most seminal mind of his generation; the mathematician-astronomer Simon Newcomb; the Leipzig Semitic scholar Paul Haupt; the economist Richard T. Ely; and the psychologist G. Stanley Hall, whose departure to the presidency of the new Clark University in 1888 carried a number of Hopkins colleagues with him. The gentle poet and musician Sidney Lanier, who joined the faculty in 1879 to lecture on Shakespeare, the English novel, and a highly original theory of prosody, may have been one of the first 'writers in residence'."

Some other early Hopkins scholars of note were Woodrow Wilson, who earned a Ph.D., Nobel Prize-winning geneticist Thomas Hunt Morgan, Frederick Jackson Turner, John Dewey, Thorstein Veblen, Maurice Bloomfield, and three pioneer women in American higher education: Christine Ladd-Franklin, M. Carey Thomas, and the first woman to be awarded a Hopkins doctorate, Florence Bascom. It was a period of great intellectual excitement—"a dawn," as Josiah Royce wrote, "wherein 'twas bliss to be alive."

* * *

Gilman's creation of a university which regarded knowledge as a dynamic force in human affairs rather than as a historical monument was a tremendous success, mainly because it filled such a pressing need in American education. Many institutions copied the Hopkins model with its emphasis on advanced study and graduate research. By the time the University reached the half-century mark, Hopkins scholars held hundreds of teaching posts at other institutions, and it had contributed nearly a quarter of the listings in *American Men of Science* and nearly a fifth of the members of the National Academy of Sciences.

The Hopkins influence was also spread through the printed word. Gilman understood the importance of publication, and almost from the beginning he saw that the results of his faculty's investigations were made known to the rest of the academic world. Hopkins quickly became a center for new scholarly journals, most of which, such as the *American Journal of Mathematics,* were the pioneer publications in their fields. They included the *American Chemical Journal,* the *American Journal of Philology, Johns Hopkins University Studies in Historical and Political Science, Modern Language*

Henry A. Rowland, a member of the original faculty and first professor of physics, established a long tradition of research in physical optics at Johns Hopkins, a field in which the University is still preeminent.

Notes, and the *American Journal of Archaeology.* These efforts led to the establishment in 1878 of a central publications agency—later known as the Johns Hopkins University Press—which also served as a model for institutional presses that followed.

Not to be neglected are the innovations in undergraduate education that the University fostered in its early years. Among the most important was the "group system," a set of

During his seven years as professor of psychology at Johns Hopkins (1881-1888), G. Stanley Hall founded the American Journal of Psychology *and established the first formal psychology research laboratory in the United States. Among his students was philosopher-educator John Dewey.*

seven coherent combinations of curricula designed to meet the needs of individual students. Hopkins was also first to develop a system of faculty advisers to help undergraduates deal with the exceptional degree of freedom they had in an institution where rules and regulations were remarkably absent. Both of these developments, along with a disposition to allow capable students to proceed at their own pace toward advanced degrees, materialized repeatedly in different forms in the University's subsequent evolution.

* * *

When it came to the establishment of the new University's medical component, President Gilman and the trustees proceeded with deliberate care, for they realized that the lowly state of 19th century American medical education demanded the same kind of boldness and creative thinking that had gone into the development of the arts and sciences.

Characteristically, Gilman sought the help of two of the best minds in medicine of the day, John Shaw Billings and William H. Welch. Billings, while overseeing the Surgeon General's Library, served as chief adviser to the Hopkins trustees on design and construction. He was responsible for the innovative pavilion design of what came to be the country's first modern teaching hospital and also espoused the primary concept that the founder had set forth: namely, that the function of the University and Hospital should be intimately related to the goals of the School of Medicine.

At the same time, Welch, appointed in 1884 as first professor of pathology, was formulating long overdue reforms in medical education. Welch and Billings developed the first medical residency system in the United States and, along with Remsen and Martin from the science faculty, designed the first pre-medical course in America, a rigorous four-year program. They also established coherent relationships between the pre-clinical and clinical sciences and among patient care, teaching, and research.

By the time the Hospital opened in 1889, other major appointments had been made, including William Osler as physician-in-chief, William S. Halsted as surgeon-in-chief, and Howard A. Kelly as gynecologist and obstetrician. These, together with Welch, were "The Four Doctors" immortalized in John Singer Sargent's painting who played a major role in revolutionizing medical education in the United States.

The formal establishment of the School of Medicine was delayed for a number of years because of a precarious financial situation that developed for the University in the late

"The Four Doctors," a famous John Singer Sargent painting, was presented to the University in 1905 by Mary Elizabeth Garrett. It shows William H. Welch, first professor of pathology; William Osler, physician-in-chief; William S. Halsted, surgeon-in-chief; and Howard A. Kelly, gynecologist and obstetrician. Together, they guided early Hopkins medicine into revolutionary pathways and ushered in the modern era of research and comprehensive patient care.

1880s. The problem was substantially resolved in 1892 through the efforts of the Women's Medical Fund, led by Mary Elizabeth Garrett, M. Carey Thomas, Elizabeth King, Mary Gwinn, and Julia Rogers. Ms. Garrett's generous contribution of $354,764 boosted the fund total to $500,000, which was offered on condition that women be admitted to the new School on the same basis as men, and that the highest academic standards be maintained—a major factor in the part subsequently played by the School of Medicine in reshaping medical education in the United States. The conditions were accepted by the trustees and, in 1893, with Dr. Welch as its dean, the School of Medicine accepted its first students. Among the women who subsequently took advantage of the unusual Hopkins policy were Florence Sabin, Phyllis Greenacre, Helen Taussig, and Gertrude Stein.

* * *

Fears that the new School's requirement of a bachelor's degree for admission and its other radically new high standards would result in a dearth of students proved to be unjustified. Superior students were in fact attracted to Hopkins simply because it did maintain high standards.

Within a few years, a basic curriculum had been established. Building upon an undergraduate education that included training in basic sciences, medical students in their first two years were required to develop a thorough understanding of subjects fundamental to clinical medicine—anatomy, pathology, physiology, and pharmacology. In the third and fourth years, students left the lecture halls and laboratories to gain practical experience in the wards and clinics of the Hospital. In making medical students in their clinical years an integral part of the Hospital staff, the School of Medicine embarked on a course which was novel in the 1890s but which quickly became standard practice.

Another of the School's major contributions was the promulgation of the "full-time" principle. As early as 1884, nine years before the School of Medicine opened, the University trustees made it clear that professorships in the pre-clinical medical sciences would be strictly full-time. This meant that holders of pre-clinical chairs would be required to devote themselves entirely to teaching and research without the distractions of private practice. Again, this was a Hopkins innovation that came to be taken for granted in all first-rate medical schools.

In 1914, after years of debate, another dramatic step was taken by the School in placing its main clinical chairs on a full-time basis. The medical faculty was by no means unanimous in support of this policy—Drs. Osler and Kelly were opposed on the grounds that it could convert clinicians into austere scientists largely removed from the humanizing doctor-patient relationship. Only Dr. Welch, with all his prestige and influence, could successfully launch such an experiment. Aided by a grant from the General Education Board, full-time professorships were established in medicine, surgery, pediatrics, and eventually in other departments. Again,

14

Biochemist John Jacob Abel, who headed the Department of Pharmacology at Johns Hopkins from 1893 to 1932, conducted pioneering studies of the isolation of hormones of the endocrine system and began work on one of the first artificial kidneys.

the example set by Hopkins was copied by other progressive medical schools.

The influence exerted by Hopkins in this case had an even broader significance, both to the University and to American philanthropy. As described by Dr. Macksey: "...it was not until support was available from the Rockefeller-funded General Education Board that the clinical services were gradually converted to full-time appointments. The example of the new medical school had, in fact, been instrumental in bringing in Rockefeller wealth into the just emerging era of medical philanthropy. The impact of Osler's *Principles and Practice* on the Rev. Frederick T. Gates, Rockefeller's principal adviser, served to inspire a massive program in aid of medical education and research. Gates turned to an early Hopkins arts graduate, Abraham Flexner, who introduced him to Welch, the medical statesman who would determine the course of such support for the next three decades." Welch was president of the board of the Rockefeller Institute for Medical Research when it opened in 1904. Flexner, in 1910, under Carnegie Foundation sponsorship, published the influential report, *Medical Education in the U.S. and Canada,* that confirmed the urgent need for reform and suggested the Hopkins model as a national standard.

The strong impetus provided by The Four Doctors and their early colleagues—J.W. Williams in obstetrics, W.S. Thayer in internal medicine, John J. Abel in pharmacology, Franklin P. Mall in anatomy, and William H. Howell in physiology— was transmitted easily to a second generation of medical pioneers. In surgery, the tradition of Dr. Halsted was carried on by J.M.T. Finney, Harvey Cushing, Walter Dandy, and Samuel Crowe. Kelly's work was furthered by Hunter Robb, T.S. Cullen, and Guy Hunner. In research, Nobel laureates George H. Whipple and Joseph Erlanger extended Welch's example, while Welch's early students Jesse Lazear and Walter Reed developed the emerging fields of public health and epidemiology.

* * *

Volumes would be needed to tell the full story of the contributions of Johns Hopkins over the years to the advancement of medical science. Many of these achievements first appeared in such publications as the *Bulletin of the Johns Hopkins Hospital,* a joint enterprise of the Hospital and the School of Medicine, the *Journal of Pharmacology,* and the *Journal of Experimental Medicine,* which had its genesis at Johns Hopkins in 1896. Beginning with Dr. Osler's great work, *Principles and Practice of Medicine,* and Howard Kelly's influential *Operative Gynecology,* a stream of basic medical texts in such fields as obstetrics, pediatrics, pathology, and physiology emanated from East Baltimore, extending the influence of the School of Medicine throughout the world.

Since its establishment, the School has produced hundreds of full professors and several thousand other teachers who have served on the faculties of more than 50 medical schools

A 1901 faculty photograph shows President Gilman, seated in the center, along with several members of the original 1876 faculty, also in the front row. They are Basil L. Gildersleeve (fourth from left), Ira Remsen (fourth from right), and Henry A. Rowland (third from right). Three of the medical faculty's original "Four Doctors" are also shown: William H. Welch (seated, second from right), William S. Halsted (second row, third from right), and Howard A. Kelly (second row, fifth from right).

in this country and overseas. Hopkins-trained doctors were instrumental in the establishment of new medical schools as well. Six medical graduates of Hopkins have reached the summit of scientific eminence—the Nobel Prize. They are, in addition to Drs. Erlanger and Whipple, Herbert S. Gasser, F. Peyton Rous, H.K. Hartline, and most recently, Hamilton O. Smith.

Mary Elizabeth Garrett headed the Women's Medical Fund which raised $500,000 in 1892 to enable the University to open its Medical School; she personally contributed more than $350,000. The gift was conditional upon the School's accepting women on the same basis as men and maintaining unprecedentedly high academic standards.

Growing pains

The University's 25th anniversary, celebrated in February 1902, was marked with both joy and sorrow—joy that the institution had been a great success and had achieved world-wide renown, and sorrow that President Gilman had reached the end of his years of fruitful service to Hopkins. More than 80 educational institutions in the United States and Canada sent delegates to the celebration. Tributes to the accomplishments of Gilman and his colleagues were paid unstintingly by such notables as the presidents of Harvard, Yale, and the University of Chicago. Woodrow Wilson, then a professor at Princeton, expressed the appreciation of alumni for Gilman's highly successful tenure. Among the major goals that had been realized in only 25 years were an institutional emphasis on independent study and research, the training of an impressive roster of advanced scholars and teachers, the promotion of scholarly publication, the creation of an academic community that fostered interdisciplinary exchange, and the emergence of an international perspective that was to be increasingly important as the University developed.

'Methods without principles,' Gilman once remarked, create 'an excellent polytechnicum, but not a university.'

The celebration was also marked by the inauguration of Ira Remsen as the University's second president. As a member of the original faculty, Remsen had gained fame for teaching and research in chemistry and become a close friend of Gilman. Unlike Gilman, however, Remsen had little taste for administration. His presidency, which lasted until 1913, was essentially a period of consolidation.

In these years, the normal course of undergraduate instruction—a three-year program instituted by Gilman leading to the B.A. degree—was extended to four years. The original program had been based on the assumption that students admitted to the University would have received extremely high quality secondary education. The apparent deficiencies of school preparation in that era led to the adoption in 1906 of the more conventional four-year course.

Almost from the time the University opened, it had been realized that the downtown Baltimore campus would not serve its needs indefinitely. As the 19th century waned, a move to a permanent suburban location became clearly desirable, but the acquisition of a suitable site proved to be difficult. The problem was eventually solved through a combination of philanthropy and intricate negotiation in which William Keyser and other civic-minded Baltimoreans—including William Wyman, Samuel Keyser, W.H. Buckler, Julian L. White, and Francis M. Jencks—played leading roles. Together, these men presented the University with a beautiful tract of land in north Baltimore that is now the Homewood campus.

Influenced by the fact that the new location had for more than a century been the site of Homewood House, a magnificent Federal-style mansion built for the son of Charles Carroll of Carrollton, the president and board of trustees adopted its architectural style in planning new University buildings. The first major building was Gilman Hall, which was dedicated in May 1915.

* * *

President Remsen relinquished his duties in 1913 for reasons of poor health, and the trustees elected Frank Johnson Goodnow, a political scientist with a long record of public service to both the U.S. and foreign governments, as the University's third president.

One of President Goodnow's greatest contributions proved to be his wise management of finances during a period of rapid expansion at the University. During his 15-year tenure, the income of the institution increased from $500,000 to nearly $2.5 million annually, while the value of plant and endowment grew from $10 million to nearly $40 million. In the final year of his administration, 68 percent of the University's expenditures went for salaries, a figure which indicated that the Hopkins tradition of placing more value on men than on buildings and appurtenances was being upheld.

Expansion during the administration of Dr. Goodnow took place in three major new areas. Shortly before his inaugura-

William Wyman was one of a group of Baltimore philanthropists who assembled and donated a large tract of wooded land which became the University's Homewood campus.

Pathologist William H. Welch was a member of the original medical faculty, first dean of the School of Medicine, and first director of the School of Hygiene and Public Health. He is shown while on a trip to China in the early 1900s, where he helped establish Peking Union Medical College.

tion, the first laboratory of the Johns Hopkins School of Engineering had been completed at Homewood. The need for such a school in Maryland had long been realized, and the occasion of the University's move to Homewood presented an excellent opportunity for launching this important project. Spurred by public-spirited citizens and conferences with the trustees, the State Legislature appropriated $600,000 for buildings and equipment in addition to an annual appropriation of $50,000 for scholarships for Maryland residents.

The first faculty in engineering was organized in 1913. John B. Whitehead, professor of applied electricity in the Department of Physics, became professor of electrical engineering and, in 1920, the School's first dean. Other initial appointments included Charles J. Tilden, called from the University of Michigan to be professor of civil engineering, and Carl C. Thomas, of the University of Wisconsin, to be professor of mechanical engineering.

During its formative years, the School of Engineering benefited from one of Gilman's early concerns that the University might concentrate on teaching methods rather than principles. "Methods without principles," he once remarked, create "an excellent polytechnicum, but not a university." This advice was always taken seriously at Hopkins and, from its inception, the new School of Engineering placed more emphasis upon the basic sciences and cultural subjects than was the custom in the vast majority of technological institutions of the day.

* * *

Another pioneering venture was launched during the Goodnow administration. In 1915, at the behest of the General Education Board, Dr. Welch prepared a report which took cognizance of the lack of educational facilities in the fields of public health and hygiene and recommended the establishment of an institute within the framework of an existing university. The result was a substantial grant from the Rockefeller Foundation for a new Johns Hopkins institution. This was the genesis of the School of Hygiene and Public Health, which was the first of its kind in the country and, in the words of historian John C. French, "the lengthened shadow of William H. Welch."

Beginning its work in the fall of 1918 with Dr. Welch as first director, the new School fully upheld the Hopkins tradition of dynamic innovation. It quickly attracted a faculty of eminent teachers and researchers, such as Elmer V. McCollum, who, in 1922, followed his earlier identification of vitamin A with the discovery of vitamin D. Other pioneering work was done in the fields of biomedical statistics, preventive medicine, epidemiology, public health administration, microbiology, pathobiology, and sanitary engineering.

By 1922, it was evident that the School was a great success. The Rockefeller Foundation provided a substantial endowment fund in addition to a $1 million construction grant. The School's new home on Wolfe Street just east of the Hospital opened in 1926 as part of the growing Hopkins medical complex in East Baltimore. The School's influence spread rapidly across the United States and overseas through a lengthening list of graduates who served city, state, and national governments in public health positions. Students came to Baltimore from more than 60 foreign countries, and many returned to their native lands to become ministers of health or chief medical officers. Of the representatives of the 66 nations who met in New York in 1946 to draft the constitution of the World Health Organization, 34 were graduates of the School of Hygiene and Public Health.

* * *

From its earliest years, the University had recognized a special responsibility to bring educational opportunities to the people of Baltimore, at first through public lectures inaugurated by President Gilman, and later through non-credit "lesson courses." In 1909, a separate division of the University, originally known as College Courses for Teachers, was organized to provide collegiate-level instruction in the field of professional education and also in the liberal arts.

An influx of workers into Baltimore during World War I greatly heightened the demand for programs of study that could be pursued in the evenings, and, beginning in 1916, courses in business and economics were offered. Night courses for technical workers were given by the School of

Marshal Ferdinand Foch, commander-in-chief of Allied armies in World War I, was presented with an honorary degree by the University during a trip to the United States in 1921. He was one of a succession of international dignitaries who have been honored by Johns Hopkins over the years, including, in recent times, German Chancellor Helmut Schmidt, Italian President Sandro Pertini, and Japanese Prime Minister Yasuhiro Nakasone.

Engineering. The demand for such courses was sustained after the war and enrollment in evening programs continued to grow. In 1947, all of the University's evening offerings were consolidated into a new division called McCoy College in honor of John W. McCoy, an early benefactor of the University. (The name of the division was changed to the Evening College in 1965 and to the School of Continuing Studies in 1984.)

* * *

President Goodnow stepped down in July 1929. His successor was Joseph Sweetman Ames, to whom fell the task of leading the University through the difficult years of the Depression. Ames, a physicist and former student of Rowland, had been associated with Johns Hopkins continuously as professor, dean, and provost. He was highly regarded in his professional area, having been elected to the National Academy of Sciences and serving as president of the American Physical Society. He was an expert in the scientific aspects of aviation and for a quarter century served as a member of the National Advisory Committee for Aeronautics, a predecessor organization of the National Aeronautics and Space Administration, which later named a research facility in his honor. Nearly 65 years of age when he took on the presidency, Dr. Ames brought to the office a wide range of useful experience.

As was the case with most universities, Hopkins had to defer many plans for new activities and expansion in the early 1930s in order to wrestle with the financial problems created by the Depression. As income fell, deficits mounted steadily, and President Ames had the onerous task of enforcing a policy of extreme frugality. Recognizing the gravity of the situation, the University faculties met and voluntarily agreed to a 10 percent cut in their salaries. This and other measures helped, but deficits continued, amounting to more than $183,000 during President Ames' last year in office.

One of Dr. Ames' legacies was a policy that was to have long-lasting effects on a less dramatic but nonetheless important part of University life. He felt strongly that it was "most improper for an institution of learning to charge admission fees to athletic contests." His feeling led to an eventual decommercialization of athletics that characterized the Johns Hopkins program for years thereafter and brought the University unusual distinction in collegiate athletics.

* * *

President Ames retired in 1935 at age 70 and was succeeded by Isaiah Bowman, director of the American Geographical Society of New York. As a distinguished geographer, he had served the government on several occasions—as chief territorial adviser to Woodrow Wilson at the Versailles peace conference following World War I, as chairman of the National Research Council, and as vice chairman of the Science Advisory Board. Throughout his life, Dr. Bowman was a productive scholar, publishing nine books and a large number of articles, mostly in the field of geography.

The new president inherited many of the financial problems which had plagued his predecessor. While adhering to a policy of strict economy, the University launched a fundraising campaign which brought pledges of about $500,000. This effort, combined with some improvement in investment income, enabled Hopkins to deal with impending deficits with greater confidence.

Throughout his presidency, Dr. Bowman placed particular emphasis on the importance of the undergraduate component to the health of the University as a whole. Whereas President Goodnow ten years earlier had proposed a plan under which Hopkins would eventually eliminate the instruction typically given in the first two years of college and combine the work of the last two years with graduate study, few students had been found who were willing to bypass the B.A. and work directly toward an advanced degree. Dr. Bowman, in his inaugural address, asserted his "resolute intention to advance the interest, improve the quality, and bring to a high state of efficiency the Johns Hopkins College of Arts and Sciences." His declaration did much to allay the concern of many alumni who disapproved of the Goodnow plan.

Dr. Bowman also emphasized the importance of graduate study to Johns Hopkins, pointing out that the graduate school was "the most valuable, most expensive, and least under-

stood intellectual enterprise of a university." He urged continuing efforts to gain support for the kind of education that
aims at high attainments by a few rather than mediocrity for
the many.

The toll—and legacy—of world war

As the decade of the 1930s waned, the portents from Europe became increasingly ominous. For universities in America, however, the imminence of war on the Continent resulted in a quantum enrichment of intellectual talent as European scientists and humanists fled threats to their academic freedom, if not to their lives. Johns Hopkins shared in this intellectual migration, as the faculty was joined by Nobel laureates James Franck and Maria Goeppert-Mayer and by other scholars representing a wide diversity of fields: philologist Leo Spitzer, poet Pedro Salinas, physicist Franco Rasetti, and historian of medicine Owsei Temkin. The arrival at Hopkins of these and other scholars was entirely in keeping with the University's early receptivity to European intellectual trends. The influx particularly influenced and strengthened work in the humanities at Hopkins for decades to follow.

With the coming of war, the tempo of activity at the University increased. Months before the United States was involved in the conflict, college-level courses aimed at the needs of defense industries were being offered on a day and night basis, and the engineering laboratories were kept in use six days a week. Research contributing to the war effort assumed massive dimensions relative to the University's size, and included development of highly-secret techniques for the manufacture of

... the imminence of war on the Continent resulted in a quantum enrichment of intellectual talent as European scientists and humanists fled threats to their academic freedom, if not to their lives.

some critical materials used in the atomic bomb and of the use of infrared rays as a detection device. At the School of Medicine, a task force coordinated a nationwide effort to develop a synthetic substitute for the anti-malaria drug, quinine. Between 1941 and 1945, the University participated in about 100 research projects related to the war. In addition to this, some 4,500 Johns Hopkins graduates, students, and faculty served in the armed forces of the United States. One hundred and twenty-two of them lost their lives in defense of their country.

One project that originated with the war effort ultimately resulted in the establishment of a permanent new division of the University. In 1942, Johns Hopkins was asked by the Office of Scientific Research and Development to undertake research to develop what came to be known as the radio-proximity or variable-time fuze. Under strict secrecy, a laboratory was established in the Washington suburb of Silver Spring, Maryland. Work proceeded on a crash basis and by the fall of 1942, the VT fuze had been perfected to the point where production could begin. The success of the device was decisive and dramatic. In Europe, it was spectacularly effective against German V-1 "buzz bombs," and in the Battle of the Bulge, artillery was able to stem the enemy advance by employing VT-fuzed shells over roads and foxholes. In the Pacific, the device greatly increased the effectiveness of antiaircraft fire and offered some defense against suicide attacks by Japanese kamikazes.

After the war, the laboratory continued to operate as the Applied Physics Laboratory under contract with the Navy Department. In 1954, many of its activities were relocated to a rural site in Howard County, Maryland, between Baltimore and Washington. APL, as it came to be known, continued to concentrate on problems of fleet defense but moved increasingly into research relating to space investigation.

Not the least of the services rendered by Johns Hopkins during World War II was the contribution of President Bowman himself. He served the Department of State as special adviser to two secretaries, was a member of the American delegation to the Dumbarton Oaks Conference, and later served as adviser to the Secretary of State at the San Francisco conference which established the United Nations.

* * *

The end of hostilities in 1945 brought a return of students to the nation's campuses. Like most universities, Hopkins had suffered a sharp decline in enrollment during the war

William George MacCallum, professor of pathology from 1917 to 1943, was widely known for research on malaria and the functions of the parathyroid gland, and for his classic textbook on pathology.

years, but the loss was quickly made up by a tide of returning veterans who took advantage of the educational benefits of the GI Bill. Veteran enrollment peaked in 1948, when the undergraduate body totaled nearly 1,800. Graduate students that year numbered 957. Veterans predominated at both levels, lending an air of seriousness and maturity to the student body not seen in prewar classes.

Having presided over the affairs of the University for more than 13 years of depression, war, and reconversion to peace, Dr. Bowman relinquished his office in December 1948. He died in 1950 and was memorialized with a bronze bust placed at the entrance to Shriver Hall. Among the enduring academic ventures initiated during his administration was one of the country's first graduate writing programs—opened under the direction of Elliott Coleman—that evolved into the widely acclaimed Writing Seminars program.

Anna Baetjer, a member of the faculty of the School of Hygiene and Public Health for 60 years, conducted pioneering studies of bronchogenic cancer, toxic chemicals, and other problems in occupational health and environmental medicine.

During these years, the University also named its first full-time director of public relations, Lynn Poole. His achievements included tapping the new medium of television to extend the University's image, and, in 1948, the *Johns Hopkins Science Review* became the first university-affiliated educational series on network television.

* * *

In January 1949, Detlev Wulf Bronk became the sixth man to occupy the office of president of Johns Hopkins. At the time of his appointment, he was Johnson Professor of Biophysics and director of the Eldridge Reeves Johnson Foundation for Medical Physics at the University of Pennsylvania. An eminent biophysicist, Dr. Bronk had served the scientific world and the government in many capacities. His scientific interests, together with a generous gift to the University, resulted in the establishment of the Thomas C. Jenkins Department of Biophysics in 1949. To house the new department, a wing was added to the biology building, Mergenthaler Hall.

Expansion by the University into an entirely different field took place during Dr. Bronk's administration when Johns Hopkins assumed responsibility for the School of Advanced International Studies, which had been established in Washington, D.C., in 1943 by the Foreign Service Educational Foundation. Among the leading figures in international relations who were instrumental in the School's founding were Christian A. Herter, Paul Nitze, Edward Burling, and J. William Fulbright. The founders believed that the postwar world would require innovative educational and professional training in the conduct of U.S. foreign policy, and the School from its inception was concerned with the training of specialists qualified to serve government and international business. By the late 1940s, the desirability of affiliation with a major university had become apparent, and overtures were made to Johns Hopkins. The School was incorporated as a graduate division of the University in 1950.

In the summer of 1953, Dr. Bronk left Johns Hopkins to become president of the Rockefeller Institute. To allow adequate time to choose a permanent successor, the trustees persuaded a familiar figure at the Medical Institutions, Lowell J. Reed, to come out of retirement and accept the presidency on an interim basis. Dr. Reed had a long association with the School of Hygiene and Public Health, where he had served as dean. In 1946, he had been appointed vice president of the University and Hospital.

Dr. Reed's term as president witnessed the completion of three new buildings at Homewood. Shriver Hall, the gift of Alfred Jenkins Shriver of Baltimore, met a long-standing need

One of the founders of the School of Advanced International Studies was Paul H. Nitze, former Secretary of the Navy and Deputy Secretary of Defense. A University trustee from 1969 to 1979, he served in the mid-1980s on the U.S. delegation to Strategic Arms Limitation Talks in Geneva.

for a modern auditorium and additional administrative office space. Ames Hall, a memorial to Hopkins' fourth president, provided classroom and laboratory space for the departments of Electrical Engineering, Sanitary Engineering, Psychology, and Mathematics. Finally, the completion of a new dormitory building made it possible for the first time to house on campus all out-of-town undergraduate students.

In 1955, the School of Advanced International Studies opened a study center in Bologna, Italy, which was the first American graduate school in Europe for the study of international relations. It proved to be a highly successful experiment in international education.

Eisenhower years: cohesive growth

The trustees deliberated for many months and considered many candidates before unanimously endorsing Milton S. Eisenhower to be the eighth president of Johns Hopkins. Dr. Eisenhower accepted and took office in October 1956, bringing to the University a wealth of experience in service to government and higher education. During World War II he had been director of the War Relocation Authority and associate director of the Office of War Information. In 1943, he returned to his native Kansas as president of Kansas State University, a position he held until 1950 when he became Pennsylvania State University's president. Among his other activities over the years, he was chairman of the U.S. National Commission for the United Nations Educational, Scientific and Cultural Organization, a member of the President's Advisory Committee on Government Organization, chairman of the Committee on Government and Higher Education, and director of the Fund for Adult Education. At the time of his acceptance of the presidency of Hopkins, he was in Panama traveling as special ambassador to Latin America for the President of the United States.

In his inaugural address on Commemoration Day in 1957, Dr. Eisenhower asserted his conviction that Johns Hopkins "must occupy a uniquely creative role in the total complex of American higher education." Affirming his belief in the historic Hopkins mission to expand the area of man's knowledge, the new president declared:

'...Though largely responsible for multiplicity, the free university has traditionally committed itself to the search for unity—to the unceasing though sometimes unsuccessful effort to bring philosophical order out of fragmented chaos.'

Milton S. Eisenhower

"Our strength cannot be in numbers. It must be in excellence. Here must be a community of scholars who, in an environ-

Milton S. Eisenhower, who served as eighth president of Johns Hopkins from 1956 to 1967, is credited with restoring fiscal vitality to the University, fostering a spirit of cohesion among its various divisions, and restoring Hopkins to its earlier prominence in the arts and sciences. In 1971-1972, he returned to office on an interim basis as the University sought a successor to President Lincoln Gordon.

ment of courageous freedom, are constantly pushing back the dark walls of the unknown. Here must be students—undergraduate, graduate, and postdoctoral—who, inspired by association with eminent minds, strive to become extraordinary humanists, extraordinary scientists, extraordinary engineers and social scientists: leaders in whatever they do. It is in character for Johns Hopkins to fulfill this role. This has been a University dedicated to exceptional men."

* * *

Dr. Eisenhower quickly discovered that the institution for which he had accepted leadership was not in the best of health. Despite spectacular accomplishments through two world wars and a depression, and despite the presence on its faculties of some of the era's most eminent scholars and scientists, Johns Hopkins generally suffered from acute financial anemia. In 32 out of the 46 years between 1910 and 1956, expenditures had outrun income, and the continuing financial drain had taken a heavy toll. Faculty salaries, once the highest in the nation, were no longer even competitive with peer institutions. Physical facilities for many units had become outmoded. Library resources were inadequate, doctoral production was stagnant, and many faculty posts were vacant for lack of funds.

"The challenge of 1956 was not only to get Johns Hopkins moving again, but to set the proper course for the future," wrote trustees' chairman Charles S. Garland in a 1967 summary of Dr. Eisenhower's administration. "This was an enormously difficult task and a perilous one," Mr. Garland continued. "Powerful forces were tugging at the University in different directions and raising perplexing questions. To know which forces to resist and to which to respond required vision, wisdom, and imagination."

A prime example of a new force in higher education with which Hopkins and all universities had to deal was the entrance of the federal government into support on a massive scale of scientific research in private institutions. Jolted by the Soviet Union's 1957 launching of the first artificial satellite, American leaders rushed to regain the scientific and technological supremacy that the United States had long enjoyed. Hopkins benefited enormously from this effort, which spilled over into a heightened interest by many foundations in bolstering private higher education.

Along with new opportunities, however, the situation posed considerable danger. Since its inception, Johns Hopkins had chosen to pursue the qualities of smallness and excellence. But this was an era of increasing gigantism in government, in business, and in higher education. How could a small and essentially elite institution, painfully in need of additional funding, avoid the centrifugal forces that tended to push it into a variety of ventures for which money was available but which could be subversive of its essential academic freedom and independence? How, as Dr. Eisenhower graphically put it, could Johns Hopkins avoid becoming "a multiversity connected only by a common plumbing system?"

There were other, equally vexing problems. Knowledge was expanding at an incredible rate, and choices had to be made at Hopkins as to what new areas could be covered without a relatively vast expansion of faculty and physical resources. Society as a whole was placing increasing demands upon its universities to solve problems of everyday living; Hopkins had a proud tradition of service to humanity but the emphasis historically had been on basic research and teaching. "In all of this there were delicate balances to be preserved," wrote Mr. Garland, "the balance between the sciences and the humanities, between undergraduate and graduate education, between research and teaching, between mission oriented and basic research, between public and private funds, between being too small to be effective and too big to be unified. And there was the ever-present and awesome task of setting priorities, of meeting unlimited needs with limited resources, of deciding which academic fields to enter or enlarge and which to leave to others."

* * *

Fortunately, the leadership of Johns Hopkins in these crucial years ranked with the best in its history. Dr. Eisenhower was noted for a capacity to view problems with a singular clarity and from the broadest possible perspective. He was a warm, friendly, and enthusiastic man, able to communicate effectively to students, faculty, alumni, and the public his genuine sense of the greatness to which Hopkins should continue to aspire. Nowhere was his effectiveness more evident than in the restoration of financial health to Johns Hopkins. Each year between 1957 and 1967, the University's budgets were in balance. Income more than tripled during the period, and the endowment fund nearly doubled, amounting at the end of 1966 to $150 million.

Federal incentives accounted for a large measure of the renewed financial vigor experienced by Hopkins, as they did for other private universities. Between 1957 and 1966, the University's operating expenditures (excluding the Applied Physics Laboratory, which was entirely supported by government funds) rose from $16.5 million to $54.8 million. Of the latter amount, the government contributed slightly more than half, mostly in the areas of medicine, basic science, and public health.

For the University to maintain independence and academic integrity in such a circumstance was no easy matter. Part of Dr. Eisenhower's solution was a campaign to attract additional support from alumni, foundations, and other areas of the private sector. The most spectacular achievement was a 1960 award of $6 million from the Ford Foundation, the largest general purpose grant in the University's history. Hopkins was one of five universities chosen by the Foundation to receive such large-scale support to bolster the general academic enterprise. It was also a major incentive to continued development, since a condition of the grant was that Hopkins raise from other sources—not including government funds—two dollars for every dollar contributed by the Ford Foundation. Friends of the University responded magnificently, to such an extent that the Foundation soon announced an additional $6 million grant to Hopkins on the same terms. Altogether during the Eisenhower years, more than $100 million was received in private gifts and grants and, by 1967, private gift income was exceeding $10 million annually.

Improved financial health made possible the achievement of goals which would have seemed impossible a few years

Helen Brooke Taussig earned her medical degree at Johns Hopkins in 1927 and, with Alfred Blalock, opened a new era in pediatric cardiac surgery with the famous "blue baby" operation, which corrected congenital heart defects.

before. Increases in faculty salaries, one of Dr. Eisenhower's highest priorities, brought Hopkins from the "B" category in national rankings back into the "A" and "AA" ratings of the American Association of University Professors. Such advances gave the University a necessary competitive edge both in retaining distinguished senior faculty and in attracting some of the best young minds in the academic world.

* * *

Long overdue attention was also paid to the bricks-and-mortar requirements of education and research. One of Dr. Eisenhower's earliest goals was a major rejuvenation of the physical plant in each of the Hopkins divisions. In the course of his presidency, more than $50 million was spent on new construction, an amount greater than the value of the entire plant at the time of his inauguration.

At the Medical Institutions, the sights and sounds of construction were rarely absent from the late 1950s onward. Major projects, some of which were undertaken with the Hospital, included the Lowell J. Reed Residence Hall, the W. Barry Wood Basic Science Building, the Biophysics Building, the Children's Medical and Surgical Center, the Alan C. Woods Research Building of the Wilmer Institute, the Samuel W. Traylor Research Building, the Thomas B. Turner Auditorium, and three additional wings to the main building of the School of Hygiene and Public Health. On property adjacent to the Medical Institutions was built the affiliated John F. Kennedy Institute for the Habilitation of the Mentally and Physically Handicapped Child.

The needs at Homewood when Dr. Eisenhower assumed office were, if anything, more critical than those in East Baltimore. For years, the inadequacy of facilities for the sciences and engineering had blunted the University's ability to maintain its traditional leadership in research and instruction. A building program was launched in the early 1960s, its main features including an addition to Rowland Hall that doubled the size of facilities for the Department of Physics and a third wing on Mergenthaler Hall which provided badly needed space for the Department of Biology. Two new buildings were constructed just to the north of Mergenthaler and

44

View of part of the Johns Hopkins Homewood campus, site of the University's School of Arts and Sciences, G.W.C. Whiting School of

Engineering, and School of Continuing Studies. The flat-roofed building in the foreground is the Milton S. Eisenhower Library.

Remsen Halls: Dunning Hall, which housed research activities of the Department of Chemistry, and Macaulay Hall, a memorial to former provost and vice president P. Stewart Macaulay, devoted to the oceanographic program of the Department of Earth and Planetary Sciences. On Wyman Quadrangle, Barton Hall, named for former trustees' chairman Carlyle Barton, was completed in 1962, providing increased space for research in radiation and electrical engineering.

The needs of humanists and social scientists at Homewood were not neglected. Centered in Gilman Hall, the 15 departments that embraced those disciplines suffered from a dearth of library space. The Gilman stacks were stuffed to the bursting point at a time when annual accretions of books and periodicals were increasing at unprecedented rates. Planning for a new library was launched in 1957, and President Eisenhower gave library fund raising top priority. Work began even before the required $4.7 million was in hand and by the fall of 1964, a magnificent new building at the east end of the Keyser Quadrangle was open for business. In addition to providing a central location for all of the University's specialized book collections, the new library included the latest electronic and acoustic appurtenances of modern scholarship, the University's computing center, and a generous number of carrels and seminar and conference rooms. In 1965, to the applause of the entire University community, the trustees named the building the Milton S. Eisenhower Library.

With the opening of the new facility, Gilman Hall was renovated to house an undergraduate library, reading room, and other study facilities, as well as an enlarged bookstore, a post office, and a bank branch. Another welcome addition completed during this period was a new classroom building on the Wyman Quadrangle that was named for G. Wilson Shaffer, distinguished psychologist and for many years dean of the Homewood schools.

At the northern end of the Homewood campus, a new facility was opened in 1965 that brought a wealth of additional recreational opportunities to students and other members of the University community. Through the generosity of Newton H. White Jr., a new athletic center that bears his name made possible a variety of indoor recreation facilities, including a competition-size swimming pool. The Center gave a tremendous lift to the Hopkins athletic program, enhancing the University's opportunities to compete in intercollegiate sports and providing a new focus for intramural competition and individual physical development.

The building program of the Eisenhower decade extended well beyond Baltimore. In 1960, Dr. Eisenhower launched a $4.2 million drive to support a ten-year improvement program at the School of Advanced International Studies; four years later, the School opened a new building on Massachusetts Avenue in downtown Washington. In 1961, the School's center in Bologna, Italy, moved into a new building that was made possible by government funds, contributions by the citizens of Bologna, and the efforts of the center's founder, C. Grove Haines.

* * *

Balanced budgets, strong government and private financial support, and a vast improvement in the physical plant all provided essential sinew that had been lacking at Johns Hopkins for many years. However, the lifeblood of the University had always been teaching and research, and the need for academic leadership was felt as strongly when Dr. Eisenhower became president as the need for new physical facilities. The tenures of his two immediate predecessors had been short. A lack of coherence and sense of drift in academic matters had begun to pervade the institution.

President Gilman in his inaugural address, with typical perceptiveness, had said: "The truth is that most institutions are not free to build anew; they can only readjust." Gilman well understood the unique opportunity he had been handed to build anew an educational institution free of the constraints of tradition or settled habits of mind. That was no small challenge, but the one faced by Dr. Eisenhower 80 years later was perhaps even greater, to the extent that resuscitation may be more difficult than creation.

In his account, Mr. Garland proposed that the word which most accurately characterized the Eisenhower period was "cohesion." Consider Dr. Eisenhower's own description of

The School of Advanced International Studies moved into this modern building on Massachusetts Avenue in downtown Washington in 1964. In 1986, an additional building nearby was acquired to accommodate the School's expanding activities.

his concept of the basic function of a university, as expressed in his annual report for 1961:

"Of all human institutions the university has for centuries been the one most intimately concerned with the necessary accommodations between unity and multiplicity. Its contributions to multiplicity cannot be denied. In every century since the middle ages Western man has looked to the universities not simply as repositories of ancient wisdom but also as crucibles where by some mysterious alchemy the store of knowledge is increased. . . . Though largely responsible for multiplicity, the free university has traditionally committed itself to the search for unity—to the unceasing though sometimes unsuccessful effort to bring philosophical order out of fragmented chaos."

In dealing with the centrifugal forces of multiplicity for which he saw universities largely responsible, Dr. Eisenhower constantly sought principles and means by which the essential unifying purpose of an institution such as Johns Hopkins could be achieved. This was a virtually superhuman task, given not only the hundreds of academic specialties involved but also the fact that Johns Hopkins was geographically dispersed into three main campuses in two cities, not to mention satellite operations such as the Bologna Center of SAIS and research affiliates such as the Applied Physics Laboratory.

* * *

It should not be inferred that the changes that swept through the University during the Eisenhower years were the result of a one-man operation. At every stage, Dr. Eisenhower was supported by able and dedicated men, such as Dean Thomas B. Turner of the School of Medicine, Dean Ernest L. Stebbins of the School of Hygiene and Public Health, Dean G. Heberton Evans of the Faculty of Philosophy, Dean Robert H. Roy of the School of Engineering, Dean Richard A. Mumma of the Evening College, Dean Francis O. Wilcox of the School of Advanced International Studies, and Ralph E. Gibson, director of the Applied Physics Laboratory. The significant fact was that the need for greater cohesion felt by Dr. Eisenhower was shared by others at the decision-making level.

Several examples from the Homewood divisions are illustrative:

• The School of Engineering, which had long stressed basic science and principles as opposed to technical training and "how-to" courses, carried the process a step further in 1961 when it was renamed the School of Engineering Science. At the same time, the departments of Aeronautics, Civil Engineering, and Mechanical Engineering were combined into a single Department of Mechanics. The next stage of integration came in 1966. For half a century, the faculties of Philosophy and Engineering had been separate entities, but it had become increasingly apparent that there was little fundamental justification for this separation. Accordingly, the two faculties merged into a single new Faculty of Arts and Sciences. In the years following the merger, the continuing integration of disciplines unified by basic principles of investigation was seen in the creation of such departments as Earth and Planetary Sciences, Geography and Environmental Engineering, and Biomedical Engineering.

• In 1961, Dr. Eisenhower expressed his concern over problems arising from what Sir Charles Snow two years earlier had called the "two cultures" of scientists and humanists. These areas existed side by side at Homewood and between them, Dr. Eisenhower said, there existed "tension, lack of sympathy, and a vast amount of misunderstanding." To bridge this gap, he proposed the development of a "sphere of activity devoted to the history and philosophy of the natural sciences." An endowment from Willis K. Shepard that year made possible a new professorship in the history of science which three years later evolved into a separate Department of the History of Science.

• Sociology, a discipline that developed its own concepts and methodologies but borrowed liberally from many areas of the sciences and humanities, was formally recognized at Hopkins with the establishment of the Department of Social Relations. Work done in this area at the University won national acclaim in the late 1960s with the publication of James S. Coleman's landmark study of racial integration in the schools.

• With the increasing use of quantitative techniques in

nearly all fields of research, recognition of statistics as a discipline came in 1962 with the establishment of the Department of Statistics. In another integrative move ten years later, the department was absorbed into a new Department of Mathematical Sciences. A close relationship developed with the Department of Biostatistics at the School of Hygiene and Public Health, including joint faculty appointments and seminars.

• Despite a long tradition of excellence in the humanities at Hopkins, financial support for these areas became increasingly difficult to find in the 1960s, particularly with much of the federal education support dollar going to science. In many instances, teaching and research in the humanities had suffered from fund-diversion impelled by federal matching grant requirements. In his concern over this problem, Dr. Eisenhower in 1964 called upon the humanities faculty to appraise the state of their programs and determine the future course they wished to follow. After two years of self-analysis, a plan emerged, and the president asked the trustees to assign highest priority to raising $4.5 million for its implementation.

One of the plan's key features was the creation of a new Humanities Center, a quasi-departmental unit designed to further the Hopkins tradition of cross-disciplinary studies of the literatures, art, philosophy and history of Western civilization. The Center circumvented the fragmentation imposed by departmental barriers at many institutions by initiating and coordinating programs that emphasized the fundamental unity of humanistic studies. Interdisciplinary teaching and research were encouraged at every level—undergraduate, graduate, and postdoctoral.

The Humanities Center was quick to make an imprint on the Homewood intellectual scene. In 1966, the Center sponsored the first symposium in the United States on "structuralism," introducing this major current in European literary theory to American scholars. The symposium reinforced Hopkins' reputation as one of the few places in this country where theoretical aspects of Continental thought—often at odds with Anglo-American critical theory—were a subject of active interest. Among the leading participants in the conference was French theoretician Jacques Derrida, who later joined the Hopkins faculty.

In addition to such academic "spectaculars," the Center over the years remained an effective intellectual and teaching presence at Homewood and turned out scores of doctoral and postdoctoral students who carried the Hopkins tradition to colleges and universities throughout the United States and abroad.

* * *

The Medical Institutions proved to be a nest of interaction, as an extraordinary degree of cooperation became manifest among the two schools and The Johns Hopkins Hospital. The administrative instrument largely responsible for this cohesion was the Medical Planning and Development Committee, made up of the president of the University and the senior officers of the Medical Institutions. Concurrently, administrative streamlining within the two schools was working toward the same end.

A revised curriculum of medical education was introduced in 1958, the goals of which, as stated by Dean Turner in his book, *Accounting of a Stewardship,* were "to accelerate the pace of medical education, to bring greater scientific content to the entire curriculum, and to effect an overdue accommodation between the sciences and the humanities as they relate to medical education." Paralleling what had happened at Homewood in engineering, the goal was the education of scholars of medicine, not the production of medical technologists. The need to accelerate medical education was given form in a combined A.B.-M.D. program set up to admit to the School of Medicine each year a small number of exceptional students who had completed two or three years of undergraduate work.

A similar A.B.-M.A. program was developed between Arts and Sciences and the School of Advanced International Studies for a selected number of liberal arts undergraduates. After three years at Homewood, a summer of intensive work in Europe, and two years at SAIS, students in this program could earn the bachelor's degree at the end of the fourth year and the master's at the end of the fifth.

Vivien Thomas, although unable to attend college because of financial considerations, became a skilled surgical technician at Johns Hopkins and played a major role in developing the "blue baby" operation. He was presented with an honorary doctorate by the University in 1976.

In the Evening College, the pervading attraction of unifying ideas was exemplified by the introduction of a new Master of Liberal Arts program. Based on the history of ideas concept nurtured at the University since the time of philosophy professor Arthur O. Lovejoy, the program departed from the usual emphasis of part-time education on job-related training and instead provided education for those who simply wanted to broaden their intellectual horizons. It proved to be one of the most successful offerings in the division's history.

Finally, the new spirit of cooperation and coordination extended to the Applied Physics Laboratory, which traditionally had had little if any contact with other Hopkins campuses. This pattern was broken in the 1960s as collaborative efforts developed between APL and the medical and engineering faculties in Baltimore in the emerging field of biomedical engineering. There were also fruitful joint projects in the fields of radiology and ophthalmology.

* * *

Another theme which emerged in the life of the University during the 1960s is most simply described in the word "outreach," which essentially meant greater involvement with daily human problems. This ran counter to the traditional Hopkins concentration on theory and principles and even sometimes threatened the hard-won spirit of cohesion. But pressures from the "outside" world were intensifying and could not be ignored.

The Medical Institutions had always been involved with the most profound of human problems, despite their orientation toward medical scholarship and research. But, as Dean Turner wrote, the most significant development at the School of Medicine between 1957 and 1967 was "a gradually dawning understanding of the role of the Medical Institutions as a social instrument with deep obligation to the medical profession on the one hand and to society in general on the other."

As an example, in the 1960s, the School of Medicine launched a broad-scale attack on diseases affecting children. The $14 million Children's Medical and Surgical Center that opened in 1964 provided facilities for some of the most advanced work anywhere in the field of pediatrics, including a substantial addition to the capacity of the Hospital. The opening of the Kennedy Institute—administratively separate but staffed by the School of Medicine—a few years later underscored this commitment to the welfare of children. The School also established cooperative relationships with medical schools in Lebanon, Nigeria, and Peru that involved faculty exchanges designed to raise the level of medical education in developing countries. In Baltimore, the School continued to provide an array of free or low-cost medical services to East Baltimore residents, and planning was begun on a new system of comprehensive, prepaid health care for residents of the new city of Columbia, Maryland, between Baltimore and Washington.

The continuing efforts of the School of Hygiene and Public Health to raise health standards in scores of countries around the world were highlighted in 1961 by the establishment of a new Department of International Health. Also created in the early 1960s at the School were the Department of Population Dynamics, a highly controversial area at the time, and the Department of Medical Care and Hospitals, which dealt on a global basis with the crucial problem of providing adequate systems of health and medical care delivery.

Involvement of a different but no less important nature was seen at the School of Advanced International Studies. A semi-independent Washington Center of Foreign Policy Research was established in 1957 to carry on intensive studies of international relations in general and problems of American foreign policy in particular. The Center, many of whose affiliates held positions in the highest levels of government, quickly became an impressive influence on the Washington scene through its research, seminars, and roundtable discussions. SAIS also began sponsoring a series of Conferences for Corporate Executives that brought together top government officials, academicians, and businessmen for frank discussions of problems in specific areas of the world.

Faculty, students, and alumni are vital constituents of any university, and they were all given due attention during the administration of Dr. Eisenhower. In addition to the improved pay scales for faculty, their numbers were increased by several hundred University wide during the 1957-1967 period. In every case, individuals were recruited who met the highest standards of professional ability and creativeness. It became commonplace at the University for senior scholars to be expert in at least two fields, such breadth of knowledge being an invaluable asset to an institution as small as Johns Hopkins. Continued faculty quality was bolstered during these years by the creation of 13 new endowed chairs—eight at the Medical Institutions, three at Homewood, and two at SAIS.

The number of undergraduates at Homewood increased by 460 during this period to 1,768 for the 1966-1967 school year. Their academic quality also improved greatly, and by 1966 Hopkins was attracting its entering students from the top 2 percent of all secondary school graduates. The graduate student population also increased sharply during the Eisenhower decade. Enrollment at the School of Medicine rose from 300 to 360; in Hygiene and Public Health, from 156 to 320; at SAIS from 76 to 287. At Homewood, the number of doctoral candidates nearly doubled, from about 700 in 1956 to 1,370 ten years later. The number of postdoctorals in residence at the University rose from about 300 to more than 800. In relation to its total enrollment, Johns Hopkins had the highest proportion of postdoctoral students of any university in the United States.

Dr. Eisenhower well understood the importance of a loyal alumni constituency. Foundations and corporations could hardly be expected to help an institution that was not supported by its own graduates. Successful efforts were made to revitalize existing alumni groups around the country and create new ones to provide a support base in virtually every geographical region. These efforts were advanced immeasurably by the work of Osmar P. Steinwald, the University's first full-time director of alumni relations. One form of evidence of his success was seen in annual contributions, which grew from $166,000 in 1956 to more than $600,000 in 1967.

One means by which the diverse Hopkins alumni constituency was brought closer together was through the *Johns Hopkins Magazine*. Revitalized in 1950 and stamped with a unique character by editor Corbin Gwaltney (who went on to found the *Chronicle of Higher Education*), the magazine continued in the Eisenhower years under editors Ronald Wolk and Anthony Neville to garner top prizes for distinction among college and university publications. One of Dr. Eisenhower's major objectives in continued support of the magazine and of an expanded program of public relations was to broaden the national image of Johns Hopkins, which often in the past had been defined almost wholly in terms of the achievements of its medical divisions.

57

Crisis and confrontation

In September 1966, Dr. Eisenhower was 67 years old. For 40 of those years he had held positions of great responsibility in government and higher education. The last decade of leading Johns Hopkins through a period of financial restructuring and academic and physical growth had taken its toll, however, and he felt the time had come to retire. He requested that the board of trustees choose a successor and relieve him of his duties by June 30, 1967.

Over a seven-month period, a selection committee—aided by a 21-member faculty and deans committee—screened 150 candidates. The final choice was Lincoln Gordon, who, at the age of 53, became the ninth president of Johns Hopkins.

Like his predecessor, Dr. Gordon brought a wealth of experience in government and higher education. A Harvard graduate and Rhodes Scholar, he had been awarded the Ph.D. by Oxford University in recognition of his book, *The Public Corporation in Great Britain.* A political economist, he had held faculty positions at Harvard, including a prestigious chair. His public service included participation in the Marshall Plan following World War II and the Alliance for Progress. From 1961 to 1966, he served as American ambassador to Brazil, and at the time of his selection as president of Hopkins was Assistant Secretary of State for Inter-American Affairs.

Fiscal stress is like a disease which affects a university's vitals, weakening morale and spreading a pall of doubt and uncertainty. Johns Hopkins faced such a situation in the years between 1969 and 1971.

President Gordon took office on July 1, 1967. In the traditional inaugural address the following February 22, he emphasized the vast changes in higher education since Gilman's retirement in 1902. He noted that whereas in its early years Hopkins had been small and preeminent in a society where higher education was a luxury enjoyed by a few, the University had maintained its traditions of smallness, independence, and excellence into the modern age when millions looked on higher education almost as a natural right and where multiversities dotted the landscape from Maine to California.

The Gordon administration lasted just under four years,

Shriver Hall, completed in 1954 at the south end of the Homewood campus, provided a large auditorium and office space. Among the stipulations made by benefactor Alfred Jenkins Shriver was that the building contain a mural of Baltimore's ten most beautiful women who lived in his day.

from July 1967 to March 1971. These were years of great stress in American society, and the nation's colleges and universities were often pressure points. This was most apparent in growing opposition to the war in Vietnam, but there were other, quite diverse forces. The aspirations of women and blacks, the involvement of universities with military research and the Reserve Officers' Training Corps, and questions of governance and students' rights were all problems that burst upon many of the nation's most prestigious campuses in the late 1960s. Hopkins was not the cauldron of discontent that boiled over at such institutions as Columbia, Cornell, Stanford, and the University of California, being insulated to an extent by a large proportion of graduate students whose interests were more often professional than political. But there were times, chiefly at Homewood, when confrontations and meetings with activist groups were a major item on President Gordon's agenda.

One focus of campus unrest nationally and at the University was military training through ROTC (the first unit of which in the nation was established at Johns Hopkins in 1916). In the fall of 1967, the Academic Council of the Division of Arts and Sciences voted to remove academic credit from courses taught under the ROTC program. The issue receded for a time but surfaced again in the spring of 1969, along with a number of others, following a raid on the Homewood campus by a Baltimore police narcotics squad. Protesting students voiced concern over the continuance of ROTC on campus and over recruiting by military and intelligence agencies of the government and by corporations involved in defense work.

President Gordon was conciliatory but firm on principle. At an open meeting of the University community in April 1969, he strongly affirmed his belief in the free university in which all opinions had the right to compete for attention and in which the rights of both minorities and majorities were respected. He defended the recruiting and the presence of ROTC as voluntary activities that were of interest to a significant number of students.

The 1969-1970 academic year saw the peak of student protest nationally. At Johns Hopkins, Vietnam Moratorium Day on October 15, 1969, drew the participation of several thousand students and sympathizers at a rally on Keyser Quadrangle. After a group of about 50 students interrupted an Academic Council meeting with a demand that business be cancelled in the spirit of the day, the crowd marched to a downtown rally where they were joined by a small contingent from the Medical Institutions. In the evening, a large crowd gathered again on the Keyser Quadrangle for a memorial service to honor Johns Hopkins alumni who had lost their lives in Vietnam.

Other issues competed for attention throughout the academic year. One was concern that as a highly intellectually selective institution, Hopkins had neglected the needs and aspirations of minority groups, particularly in student recruiting. Although efforts had been made starting in the mid-1960s to improve this situation, by 1969, only 4.2 percent of the University's enrollment represented minority groups. The effort was stepped up, aided by the Black Graduate Students Association which sent representatives to a number of predominantly black colleges, and by the fall of 1970, the percentage of minority students enrolled had risen to 5.8.

The governance issue also came in for increased attention in 1970 with students seeking to participate in some of the key decisions in academic matters. A University Senate that included students was proposed, but the Academic Council, which had long ruled over this realm, was not enthusiastic about such a change. No real structural changes in academic governance resulted, but student input was incorporated in a number of important areas within a few years. Starting in 1971, a graduating senior was elected each year to the board of trustees for a four-year term. Students from various divisions also began serving on a Public Interest Investment Advisory Committee which advised the trustees on the voting of the University's common stock holdings. Students were also involved in planning the University's centennial celebration and in the management of a new student union.

The Applied Physics Laboratory emerged as another issue in the spring of 1970 as a group calling itself the Committee on APL argued against Hopkins' affiliation with a "$50 million-a-year partner in the military-industrial complex." The activists modified their initial demands that the University separate itself from APL but called for its conversion to "socially useful" activity. President Gordon rejected most of the committee's proposals and pointed out that APL was already expanding its work into a number of non-military areas, including health, transportation, and space research.

The climax of this year of discord came in late April when a student strike was called at Homewood and about half the undergraduates refused to attend classes. After two days of discussions with the administration, in which it was agreed to suspend military recruiting on campus unless students voted in a referendum to retain it, the strike was called off. Another wave of protest rolled over the nation's campuses in early May, following the Cambodian incursion and the shooting of students at Kent State University in Ohio. Hopkins students participated in rallies in Baltimore and Washington and Dr. Gordon co-signed a letter to President Nixon expressing alarm over "the dangers of an unprecedented alienation of America's youth."

* * *

The tumult of this time should not obscure the fact that the work of the University went on as before. There were also a number of changes of importance in the Gordon years. In October 1969, the Academic Council recommended that female undergraduates be admitted starting in the 1970-1971 school year. The idea was approved by the president and the trustees and a 93-year-old tradition of an all-male undergraduate body was broken. Alumni resistance proved to be minimal, and the feeling among faculty and students was positive, since segregation by sex seemed more anachronistic every year. Ninety women enrolled in the fall of 1970 and, aside from a few problems with housing and some complaints of a lack of special counseling and other services, most adjusted well to the University's long-standing policy of allowing students a maximum of freedom and independence. The *Johns Hopkins Magazine* reported that the new presence of women undergraduates "made surprisingly few changes in campus life." Within three years, the number of women had risen to 472 in a total student body of 2,073.

The early flickerings of an "outreach" movement at Hopkins noted earlier continued to grow and gather strength through the 1960s. While initially manifested in developments in East Baltimore, this new direction in Johns Hopkins activities showed up in non-medical activities as well. One example was the establishment in 1968 of a Center for Urban Affairs; another was the founding the following year of the Greater Homewood Community Corporation.

Supported by Ford Foundation and other private grants, the Center was designed to conduct research and training in urban problems, serving as a catalyst in bringing together expertise in urban affairs that already existed in the various schools and divisions. The Center was initially quartered at the Medical Institutions but, in 1972, was moved to Homewood and renamed the Center for Metropolitan Planning and Research. Under the direction of Jack C. Fisher, the Metro Center, as it came to be known, inaugurated a broad program of research and teaching in contemporary problems facing urban areas in the United States and abroad. Two new fellowship programs were noteworthy, one of which enabled Hopkins undergraduates to serve as interns in the offices of municipal department heads and elected officials in Baltimore City, and another which made it possible for European scholars and students of urban problems to spend time at the Center studying the problems of their cities from the perspective of the American environment.

The Greater Homewood Community Corporation was originally set up to identify neighborhood issues and develop local leadership resources in a three-and-a-half-square-mile area surrounding the campus. The organization subsequently became involved in a variety of community improvement activities, all of which helped dispel the remote ivory tower image of the University which was widely held among the neighboring population. Johns Hopkins was a partner in the Corporation's efforts through the Office of Community Affairs and through membership on the Corporation's board of directors.

Also during this period, Dr. Gordon convened a meeting to which all independent colleges in Maryland were invited to send representatives. Formed at that meeting was what

The original domed building of The Johns Hopkins Hospital stood as the centerpiece as one of the world's most modern medical complexes grew up around it. Between 1973 and 1983, more than $150 million was spent on new construction and renovation on the East Baltimore campus to support the historic roles of teaching, research, and patient care.

came to be known as MICUA, the Maryland Independent College and University Association, an organization which has as its primary task the establishment and maintenance of good relations with the State of Maryland.

Physical improvements at Homewood during these years included the construction of a large new building just south of Levering Hall to house for the first time under one roof most of the offices of the University's central administration. Completed in the summer of 1971, the building was named in honor of former trustees' chairman Charles S. Garland. In 1969, a new alumni headquarters was opened at 3211 North Charles Street across from the campus in a former residence that was donated to the University by Jacob Hain. It was later named the Steinwald Alumni House in honor of Osmar P. Steinwald.

* * *

A number of important research advances were reported during the Gordon years. At the Medical Institutions, physicians and engineers worked together in developing ultrasonic instruments for eye and brain surgery and the use of telemetry and computers to monitor hospital patients. H.K. Hartline, former chairman of the Department of Biophysics, shared the 1967 Nobel prize in medicine for work on chemical and physiological processes in the eye. In 1968, Vincent L. Gott and a surgical team performed Hopkins' first heart transplant operation. In 1969, The Johns Hopkins Hospital was the only American hospital chosen by the World Health Organization to participate in a global study of breast cancer. William B. Kouwenhoven, lecturer in surgery and former dean of the School of Engineering, was honored by the Institute of Electrical and Electronics Engineers in 1970 for developing the basis and practical means of defibrillating the heart externally and the technique of closed chest cardiac massage; three years later he received the Albert Lasker Clinical Medical Research Award for "landmark contributions to the care of cardiac patients." Also in 1970, Hopkins surgeons became the first in the United States to provide artificial hip replacements.

The School of Hygiene and Public Health in 1968 won

support from the Rockefeller Foundation for a large-scale study of schistosomiasis, or "snail fever," a disease that affected 150 million people worldwide. In 1969, a team headed by Philip E. Sartwell published a long-awaited study on the effects of oral contraceptives.

Late in 1970, the results of a five-year collaborative effort involving the Applied Physics Laboratory, the School of Medicine, and the School of Hygiene and Public Health were unveiled at a gathering of several hundred physicians, scientists, and journalists. Among the presentations were a new electrically powered artificial limb system for the upper extremities, a left-heart bypass pump which stimulated the pulsatile pattern of blood flow, a new technique for displaying three-dimensional radiographic images, and the use of a fluorescing dye in diagnosing retinal vascular system disorders.

Construction projects completed during the Gordon administration included the Ernest Lyman Stebbins Building of the School of Hygiene and Public Health in 1968. Named for the former dean, the building provided student seminar and study areas, laboratories, office and library space, and a cafeteria. Another distinguished dean emeritus was honored when the School of Medicine dedicated the Thomas B. Turner Auditorium, which provided a 750-seat auditorium, seminar rooms, and other facilities.

At the School of Advanced International Studies, a new Center of Canadian Studies was established with the aid of a $1 million grant from the William H. Donner Foundation and the Donner Canadian Foundation. It was the first graduate center in the country devoted to Canadian studies. The School marked its 25th anniversary in October 1970; the occasion featured a talk by former Secretary of State Dean Acheson.

* * *

While modern private universities are well adapted to withstand the strains of confrontation and ideological division such as those that surfaced during the Gordon years, they are less suited to cope with serious financial crises. Fiscal stress is like a disease which affects a university's vitals, weakening morale and spreading a pall of doubt and uncertainty. Johns Hopkins faced such a situation in the years between 1969 and 1971, as steadily increasing deficits brought on the gravest financial crisis since the 1930s. In fiscal 1969, the deficit was a modest but ominous $530,000. In 1970, it was an alarming $2.9 million. By 1971, it was a staggering $4.2 million.

The relatively sudden deluge of red ink was due to a complex interweaving of circumstances. A high inflation rate contributed to a persistent rise in costs for goods and services. Another element was under-recovery of indirect costs for sponsored research resulting from ever-changing accounting procedures imposed by the federal government. Still another was a sharp downturn in federal support of graduate education and research. A rapid growth in the size of the Arts and Sciences faculty and a near doubling of administrative personnel in the University played a crucial role in the developing crisis.

To some extent, the faculty and staff expansion was an outgrowth of recommendations of a long-range planning committee appointed by President Eisenhower in 1964—a time when the University's financial health was robust. Although never officially endorsed, these recommendations had considerable effect on the policies of the Gordon administration. With the benefit of hindsight, it can be suggested that the financial crisis of 1969-1971 resulted largely from implementation of the earlier recommendations even when it was clear that the necessary resources did not exist. In the years in question, 70 faculty positions were added at Homewood and the number of administrative personnel rose from 150 to 297. Total student enrollment during the period increased by only about 100. Income increased, but not at the same rate as expenditures, and the upshot was an ever-tightening financial squeeze.

Retrenchment efforts were begun in 1970, but by then it was too late to avoid piling up the greatest deficit in the institution's history, a situation that necessitated the spending of carefully husbanded reserves. There was much doubt, division, and uncertainty early in 1971, and much of this landed at the president's door. Dr. Gordon submitted his resignation to the board of trustees on March 12, and it was accepted by the executive committee. Chairman Robert D.H. Harvey, in a statement to the press, said: "The action of the executive committee was taken with great regret. Dr. Gordon's leadership spanned a period of grave crisis for American institutions of higher learning. Many problems remain for solution, but Dr. Gordon has made substantial progress in charting a course for the University's future and in overcoming its serious financial problems."

* * *

It was realized that the selection of a new president would be a time-consuming task. Meanwhile, among faculty, students, administrators, and board members, a consensus developed that the best possible course in this time of crisis would be to persuade Milton Eisenhower to come out of retirement and accept the presidency on an interim basis. At the age of 71, he was extremely reluctant to take on this arduous task, but his sense of duty and dedication to the University were strong, and he agreed to return for a limited period. His appointment was announced on March 25 and took effect April 5. The crisis had not destroyed everyone's sense of humor—campus wags referred to Dr. Eisenhower's reassumption of the presidency as the Second Coming.

Ten days after returning to office, Dr. Eisenhower addressed a special convocation of faculty, students, and staff which filled the Shriver Hall auditorium to overflowing. Enthusiasm ran high in an audience which realized how much intelligence and zeal this man had devoted to the welfare of Johns Hopkins. Dr. Eisenhower in no way minimized the problems facing the institution. He pointed out that the cash deficit for fiscal 1971 would be more than $4.5 million, and proceeded to outline a number of measures designed to bring the runaway financial situation under control. They included painful but necessary budget cuts that involved administrative offices, academic departments, and auxiliary enterprises.

Looking ahead, he proposed a substantial increase in the size of the undergraduate program, noting that since 1967 the student-faculty ratio had dropped from about 13:1 to 10:1. Citing the need for youth and female representation on the board of trustees, Dr. Eisenhower announced several by-law changes designed to achieve that end. He also promised no tuition increase during his interim term and stressed his strong desire that an adequate student union be provided for the Homewood campus. As his address neared an end, he said: "My energy is not what it was when I left here. But now that I have returned, my reluctance is forgotten and I shall personally do all I can to forward the interests of this distinguished institution for the short time I am here." The audience responded with a standing ovation.

* * *

In spite of what he had said, in the ten months of his second presidency, Dr. Eisenhower demonstrated that his energy had suffered no noticeable diminution. In this time, as the *Johns Hopkins Magazine* expressed it, ". . . the University community realized that in his efforts to get the University moving again the veteran administrator had produced nothing short of a miracle." In the financial sphere, there were these accomplishments: the board of trustees pledged $1.2 million as a tribute to Dr. Eisenhower's leadership; 12 corporations and foundations gave nearly $4 million to support a variety of programs; the State of Maryland, following an initiative developed by President Gordon, granted $800,000 to the School of Medicine and $355,000 to Arts and Sciences; alumni contributed a record $1,251,400; and a new chair in the History of Art was endowed through a $750,000 gift from the William R. Kennan Jr. Charitable Trust.

At the Medical Institutions, Russell H. Morgan succeeded David E. Rogers as dean of the School of Medicine in November 1971. Dr. Rogers, who had become dean upon the retirement of Dean Turner in 1968, presided over the school at a time when "outreach" moved into high gear. A prepaid health care program was established by Johns Hopkins in Columbia, Maryland, and this was soon followed by a similar program in East Baltimore. These were pioneering ventures in a new concept of health care delivery that was to assume increasing importance and acceptance in the 1970s and beyond. In another new venture, the trustees in September 1971 approved the creation of a new school of allied health sciences, including nursing, mental health counseling, medical and radiological technology, and other paramedical disciplines.

* * *

From the beginning of Dr. Eisenhower's second presidency, a trustees' search committee assisted by an advisory group made up of faculty, students, and alumni was hard at work screening scores of potential candidates for the University presidency. By early 1972, it was apparent that an announcement was near. In mid-January, Dr. Eisenhower issued a farewell statement summarizing the past ten months and noting that on the crucial financial front, the deficit for 1972 would be less than the $2.4 million budgeted and that the budgeted deficit for fiscal 1973 was down to $1.1 million. (The actual deficit for 1972 was less than $1.8 million, and that for 1973 was only $700,000.)

In his final words, Dr. Eisenhower summed up his feelings on his second presidency: "Candidly, I was quite content when I left here on June 30, 1967. It is no secret that I did not wish to return. When my conscience overcame my common sense and I acceded to the urgings of trustees and faculty members to serve again on an interim basis, I experienced what I was sure would be inevitable. I had to do mean things nearly every day, things that made me feel wretched. But with equal candor I say that if I now moved back to March 25, 1971, I would do again precisely what I have done. I would accept, I would have heartwarming cooperation, and I would leave about ten months later with a feeling of genuine friendship for all of you."

72

Steven Muller became tenth president of Johns Hopkins in 1972. His tenure has seen such academic advances as the opening of new engineering and nursing schools and an affiliation with Baltimore's Peabody Institute, as well as expansion of the University's educational activities in Europe and the Far East. Other achievements include strengthening the University's financial foundation and modernizing the physical plant through a major construction and renovation program.

The Muller era begins

On January 20, 1972, the trustees elected Steven Muller the tenth president of Johns Hopkins. Dr. Muller, who took office on February 1, had come to the University as provost at the beginning of Dr. Eisenhower's interim presidency—several months earlier than originally planned, at Dr. Eisenhower's urging. Dr. Muller quickly impressed faculty, students, and administrators alike with his highly articulate nature, his keen grasp of the University's problems, and his energetic and incisive approach to their solution.

A 1948 graduate of the University of California, Dr. Muller was a Rhodes Scholar from 1949 to 1951. He received his Ph.D. from Cornell in 1958 and was director of the Cornell Center for International Studies from 1961 to 1966. For the next five years, he was Cornell's vice president for public affairs. At 44, he became the youngest president of Johns Hopkins since Daniel Coit Gilman.

In his inaugural address on February 22, 1972, Dr. Muller touched on several themes. "Our heritage at Hopkins is that we are small and superb," he asserted. "We must continue to earn that reputation." He expressed his convictions about the advantages of being a private institution: "We have at least the freedom to choose among alternatives, restricted as that choice may be, rather than to have our decisions dictated to us by public bodies." The new president also emphasized the historic mission of the true university: "Universities ... are ... profoundly human in the natural or animal sense. Into them pour the young, full of pas-

'It is time for major private institutions in this country to say aloud that they intend to survive, that they will survive, and by doing so set an example for all privately funded institutions be they schools, churches, hospitals, symphonies, or universities.'

Steven Muller

sion and natural appetites. The same passions and appetites course through the rest of us. No man is pure reason. A university therefore is a deeply human organism in which reason and nature strive together as in mankind itself. Sometimes the flesh is martyred by reason, sometimes reason is martyred by human passion. Passion in the service of reason can lead to the utmost in human achievement. Reason in the service of passion can lead to the torment of men and women by each other. At universities, reason has a special priority."

As Dr. Muller assumed the presidency, The Johns Hopkins University presented the picture of an incredibly complex social institution totally committed to its original mission of teaching and research but existing in a world that bore little resemblance to that of Daniel Coit Gilman and his founding faculty. How the new administration responded to that environment was to be a key factor in the shaping of the University's future—both immediate and long term.

Topping the agenda of concern was the financial health of the institution—somewhat improved from just a year earlier but still a real threat to the continuation of the Johns Hopkins Institutions in the form in which they had evolved. Dr. Muller and his staff attacked the problem with determination and imagination, and their success will be described in a following section.

An administrative change that was to be of immense significance in both the financial struggle and the general development of the University was announced in September 1972. Effective October 1, Steven Muller would become president of The Johns Hopkins Hospital as well as president of the University, thus binding the two institutions together under a single leadership for the first time since President Gilman acted briefly as chief executive of the Hospital in 1889. William E. McGuirk Jr., chairman of the Hospital trustees, observed that the two institutions had been intimately associated since their founding, and that "the rapid and extensive development of joint School of Medicine and Hospital programs in recent years makes it highly appropriate that the presidencies of the institutions now be combined."

Recognizing the virtual impossibility of administering both institutions on a day-to-day basis, President Muller appointed Robert M. Heyssel, professor of medicine and former director of the Office of Health Care Programs, as executive vice-president and director of the Hospital. Another change in the administrative structure of the medical institutions was made early the following year, when Russell H. Morgan, dean of the School of Medicine since 1971, became vice president for the health divisions.

A clear demonstration of the value of the joint presidency was quickly at hand. On Commemoration Day in 1973, President Muller announced the launching of the largest and most significant fund-raising campaign in the history of the Johns Hopkins institutions. A joint endeavor of the University and the Hospital, the $100 million campaign was called "Hopkins Hundreds" to symbolize two of the drive's major objectives: to bring to 100 the number of permanently endowed professorial chairs throughout the University, and to make possible a badly needed rebuilding and renovation program at the Hospital.

Specifically, the goals included the raising of $20 million in private funds for the Hospital (with another $80 million to be borrowed and repaid out of income from patient care) and $50 million to provide 50 new named professorships. Other objectives included $6 million in program support for the new School of Health Services, $4 million to support the educational programs of the School of Medicine and the School of Hygiene and Public Health, $15 million in additional endowment and new teaching and research facilities for the Homewood divisions, and $3 million for library expansion, renovation of existing facilities, and student support endowment at the School of Advanced International Studies.

In announcing the campaign, President Muller made his determination clear: "It is time for major private institutions in this country to say aloud that they intend to survive, that they will survive, and by doing so set an example for all privately funded institutions be they schools, churches, hospitals, symphonies, or universities."

One year later on Commemoration Day, 1974, Dr. Muller was able to announce that the effort to date had been crowned with tremendous success. The halfway mark had been reached, as slightly more than $50 million had been raised or pledged in one of the most successful 12-month efforts in the history of American philanthropy. More than $10 million had been committed by trustees of the University and Hospital alone.

* * *

The intense fund-raising activity was carried on side-by-side with the University's day-to-day business. At Homewood, student activities gave evidence of new vitality. The student-managed Milton S. Eisenhower Symposium, inaugurated in 1967 and named in honor of the former president, attracted growing attention and respect. The symposium of 1972 had as its theme, "Creativity: The Moving Force of Society," and attracted the talents of such figures as critic Clive Barnes, psychologist Jean Piaget, sociologist Nathan Glazer, and composer Aaron Copland. In 1973, the event dealt with the well-chosen topic, "Living with Change," which brought to the Shriver Hall stage the insights of engineer-philosopher R. Buckminster Fuller, theologian Harvey Cox, and author Isaac Asimov.

In 1972, Homewood undergraduates staged a spring fair which they called "3400 on Stage," a reference to the University's address, 3400 North Charles Street. This became a highly popular annual event, featuring entertainment, food, arts and crafts, music, drama, exhibits, and even fireworks. Aside from the fun they provided, these April festivals did much to acquaint campus neighbors and thousands of other Baltimoreans with the mission and facilities of the University's Homewood campus.

The increasing numbers and importance of women on the Homewood campus were cause for another kind of celebration during this period. To mark the graduation of the first four-year coeducational class in 1974, students organized "Next Step: A Festival of Women," which featured talks by actress Jane Fonda and poet Anne Sexton, among others. During that academic year, there were 472 female undergraduate and 246 female graduate students enrolled at Homewood, constituting 23 percent and 26 percent of these categories, respectively. A December 1973 status report on women in the Arts and Sciences division showed that women held five places on the Student Council, the presidency of the Debate Council, and representation on several policy-making and problem-solving committees. Women were also eligible for ROTC scholarships and second lieutenant commissions in the Army.

* * *

These developments were all viewed with great satisfaction by Dr. Muller, for a long-standing need to improve the quality of student life at Hopkins was not lost amid his concern for the future financial health of the institution. Following a recommendation of a blue ribbon Committee on Undergraduate Education, the president appointed a dean of students for the division of Arts and Sciences in the spring of 1972 with responsibility for most areas of non-academic affairs, including student counseling, health services and the psychological clinic, student activities, and the physical education program.

Also appointed was a director of the new Hopkins Union, which was completed in the summer of 1974, fulfilling the heart-felt desire expressed by Dr. Eisenhower in 1971. This handsome building in modern style provided meeting rooms, offices for various student organizations, a small theater, and a rathskeller. The adjoining Levering Hall was also completely renovated, including the Great Hall, cafeteria, and lobby, where a central information center to serve the entire Homewood community was set up.

* * *

The attention paid in the early 1970s to such housekeeping matters as the University's financial health and the betterment of the quality of student life did not detract from the main mission of the institution. That always had been and continued to be the nurturing of the life of the mind. Some examples of scholarship and research during this period follow.

In the summer of 1972, a team led by Egyptologist Hans Goedicke, professor of Near Eastern studies, excavated an ancient cemetery near the Great Pyramid at Giza. From this

Homewood, a Federal-style mansion built in 1801 by Charles Carroll of Carrollton—a signer of the Declaration of Independence—as a wedding gift for his son, gave the University's North Baltimore campus its name and set the architectural style of campus buildings for decades to come. The house was designated a National Historic Landmark in 1976 and, in the mid-1980s, was restored for use as a public museum.

and regular subsequent expeditions, Dr. Goedicke learned much about life in ancient Egypt and how the huge pyramids were constructed. His research furthermore revealed new insights into such Biblical phenomena as the swallowing up of the pharaoh's troops by a giant tidal wave during the Exodus.

Three members of the Homewood faculty were elected to the National Academy of Sciences in 1972, bringing to 15 the number of Johns Hopkins faculty in that prestigious organization. The new members were James S. Coleman, professor of social relations; Hans P. Eugster, professor of geology; and Saul Roseman, professor of biology. A two-volume biography of the English artist Hogarth by English Department Chairman Ronald Paulson received international acclaim and a National Book Award citation.

In the fall of 1972, the Department of Geography and Environmental Engineering received a $1.2 million grant from the Edison Electric Institute to continue a long-term study of thermal pollution, particularly the effects of power plant warm water discharges on living organisms in nearby waters. This work continued a long tradition in water resources research at Homewood that was personified by men like Abel Wolman and John C. Geyer.

Early the following year, the University announced that alumnus and distinguished novelist John Barth was returning to Johns Hopkins with a joint appointment in the Writing Seminars and the Department of English. Also joining the English faculty that year was Hugh Kenner, an internationally known critic, author, and expert on T.S. Eliot, James Joyce, Samuel Beckett, and Ezra Pound. In other research, a young Hopkins paleobiologist, Steven Stanley, developed a persuasive explanation for the explosive speed on a geologic time scale of the development of higher life forms during the Cambrian Period. James F. Bell, professor of solid mechanics, became the first person to write, without collaboration, an entire volume in the *Handbuch der Physik* series, a primary reference source used by scientists all over the world.

Further honors won by Homewood faculty during this period included the election of Maurice Mandelbaum, Andrew W. Mellon Professor of Philosophy, to the American Academy of Arts and Sciences. Clifford Truesdell, professor of rational mechanics, was appointed to the Lincean Professorship, one of Italy's highest academic honors. Honorary degrees from prestigious European universities were won by biophysicist Martin G. Larrabee and Francis J. Pettijohn, professor emeritus of Earth and Planetary Sciences, both National Academy of Sciences members. Newly elected to the Academy in 1973 were Donald D. Brown and Robert G. Parr, along with Victor A. McKusick and Helen B. Taussig of the Medical Institutions.

* * *

In developments in other academic divisions of the University in the early years of President Muller's administration, the Evening College made several significant changes in curriculum and structure. The school expanded its graduate degree offerings, especially in the education area in response to the needs of education specialists in reading, counseling and guidance, and adult education. Graduate-level programs were approved in business and administrative science. A Division of Special Programs was created to handle multidisciplinary and interdivisional degree programs, such as the M.S. in Urban Planning.

* * *

Authorized in 1971, the School of Health Services opened in East Baltimore in 1973 under the leadership of Dean Malcolm Peterson with a class of 35 students. The School had been conceived in response to changing patterns in the delivery of health care nationally and was designed to prepare health associates as technicians capable of dealing with common health problems of children, adults, and families. The fledgling School received a powerful boost in its opening year in the form of a $3 million grant from the Robert Wood Johnson Foundation. The initial curriculum was designed to provide the third and fourth years of a baccalaureate degree program and emphasized human biology, the social sciences, the humanities, as well as clinical skills.

* * *

Research at the School of Medicine continued at the productive pace that had come to be associated with the Medical Institutions over the years. In March 1973, it was announced that Mackenzie Walser, professor of pharmacology and experimental therapeutics, had developed a new drug treatment for chronic kidney failure which could replace or delay the need for renal dialysis. The new treatment employed synthetic drugs combined with a low-protein diet to provide necessary nourishment without producing waste products kidneys could not remove.

An example of the fruitful cooperation that was developing between scientists at the medical institutions and the Applied Physics Laboratory was a revolutionary rechargeable heart pacemaker. The result of five years of collaborative research between Robert Fischell, an APL physicist, and Kenneth B. Lewis, assistant professor of medicine, the pacemaker was about the size of a flat cigarette lighter. It was surgically implanted and powered by a special battery that could be periodically recharged through the patient's skin without further surgery. The device, which was projected to have a useful life of at least 20 years, was a clear example of the ways in which funds spent to develop space technology could benefit medicine, since the crucial component had grown out of APL's experience in building batteries for spacecraft.

* * *

In the School of Hygiene and Public Health, a precarious financial situation which had existed in 1972 was overcome by the skillful efforts of Dean John C. Hume and his associates. There was also some restructuring within the School, as a new Department of Environmental Health Sciences was established to consolidate teaching and research that had long been conducted in other departments in five separate areas.

Noteworthy research during this period included work in the Department of Population Dynamics, where Melvin Zelnik and John Kantner conducted highly influential studies of the sexual habits of American teenagers. Their conclusions pointed up the need for more adequate and far-reaching programs of sex education. The department was also intimately involved in helping Bangladesh, Taiwan, Turkey, and

Pakistan to develop and implement their own family planning programs.

* * *

At the School of Advanced International Studies, Robert E. Osgood succeeded Francis O. Wilcox as dean in 1973. Dr. Osgood, who joined the SAIS faculty in 1961, had been director of the Washington Center of Foreign Policy Research. Another administrative change took place at the Bologna Center in 1972, when Simon Serfaty, a SAIS alumnus, was appointed director upon the retirement of founder C. Grove Haines.

Two important developments at SAIS during this period deserve attention. The Ocean Policy Project was established in 1972 with a grant from the National Science Foundation. Conducted under the auspices of the Washington Center of Foreign Policy Research, the project focused research efforts on the policy options available to the United States in the Third United Nations Conference on the Law of the Sea.

Following 1981 Commencement exercises, President Steven Muller traded his mortarboard for less conventional headgear with the inscription Go For 4 Jays, which symbolized Hopkins' hopes for a fourth straight NCAA lacrosse title. Posing with him are four members of the graduating class, including Michael S. Steele, right, who had just been named a young trustee.

Another offshoot of the Center of Foreign Policy Research was the Institute of International Social Science Research, established in 1973 and supported by an endowment from the Rockefeller Brothers Fund. The institute utilized opinion-polling techniques at both public and private levels in the preparation of literature on the psychological dynamics that influence political and social behavior in the United States and other countries.

* * *

Thus the decade of the 1970s moved toward midpoint. Financial pressure eased, but only a little. Academic departments maintained their high standards, but with growing difficulty as little money was available for salary increases, new equipment, or better physical facilities. These problems were being addressed, but it was taking time to see results. Morale at Johns Hopkins had seen loftier heights.

Early on a cold Christmas Eve morning in 1973 at Baltimore's Green Mount Cemetery, President Muller led a small delegation to the grave where the University's founder had been buried a century before. Those taking part in a simple wreath-laying ceremony included trustees' chairman Robert D.H. Harvey, Baltimore Mayor William Donald Schaefer, members of the University and Hospital administrations, and members of the Hopkins family. Said Dr. Muller: "As we salute a life that brought so much to life, we dedicate ourselves anew to the spirit of compassion and love of mankind that is the most enduring and endearing part of our founding. We thank and cherish the memory of Mr. Johns Hopkins."

Just ahead lay the University's centennial year. It was an experience that none who went through it could easily forget, and one that was to have far greater impact on the institution than the simple observing of the passage of a century.

Centennial

"It is altogether appropriate that the 100th anniversary of Johns Hopkins, which provided the model for the nation's graduate-oriented research universities, will bring together some of the finest minds in the civilized world to consider questions that are among the most beguiling to present-day scholars."

In those words, President Muller in the spring of 1975 expressed the theme that had been building through five years of planning for the biggest celebration in the University's history. And what a celebration it was! In addition to nearly two dozen major symposia that did indeed bring to Baltimore some of the world's leading scholars and scientists, there was a banquet, a ball, a picnic, a centennial ode, a centennial sculpture, a centennial symbol, speeches, reflections, predictions, and even a protest that served as a real-world counterpoint to the theoretical ponderings of many of the academic events. Climaxing this year-long celebration of the past was news of major significance to the University's future —the successful completion of the Hopkins Hundreds campaign.

The fact that this tidal wave of events—which involved dozens of Nobel laureates, university presidents, and other international figures as well as Hopkins faculty, students, trustees, staff, and alumni —went off virtually without a flaw is a tribute to hard work by a lot of University people and to the planning effort headed by Ferdinand Hamburger Jr. A former undergraduate, graduate student, faculty member, and long-time chairman of the Department of Electrical Engineering, Dr. Hamburger was appointed

On the Shriver steps in a drizzle between conference papers, Dean George E. Owen was explicit about what one might wish to recapture. 'The Golden Age,' he pronounced, 'was when a man could make his own apparatus. And lift it.'

by President Gordon in 1969 to serve as director of centennial planning.

Centennial events were spread throughout the 1975-1976 academic year, with formal opening ceremonies on September 10, 1975, on the quadrangle in front of Gilman Hall. Under a brilliant sun, Maryland Governor Marvin Mandel and Mayor Schaefer read proclamations acclaiming the University's contributions to the city and state. The principal speaker, appropriately, was the man who had twice served Johns Hopkins as president, Milton S. Eisenhower. Also at the opening ceremony, a magnificent centennial sculpture—an intriguing abstract work formed of a swirl of polished steel bars—was formally accepted. The work of young American artist David Lee Brown, the sculpture was a gift to the University from alumnus and trustee Robert H. Levi and his wife, Ryda.

* * *

The idea behind the impressive series of symposia which constituted the heart of the centennial observance was to bring together leading contemporary experts to discuss areas in which Johns Hopkins scholars and scientists had made significant contributions over the years. Another major concern was current issues facing higher education in America. Thus, such disciplines as psychology, continuing education, semiotics, genetics, nutrition, biomedical engineering, and cosmology were among those prominently treated.

One of the main events was described in the May 1976 "Centennial" issue of the *Johns Hopkins Magazine* by Hugh Kenner, Andrew W. Mellon Professor in the Humanities. Dr. Kenner wrote his impressions of the Rowland-Wood Symposium on Physical Optics, held in November 1975. It honored two of the University's most illustrious scientists: Henry A. Rowland, first professor of physics, and Robert W. Wood, an ingenious and often theatrical experimenter who carried on Rowland's tradition of pioneering work in optics and spectroscopy. A display of more than 100 historically precious items relating to their work centered around an enormously important scientific tool perfected by Rowland—diffraction gratings, polished glass plates upon which were ruled as many as 43,000 precisely-spaced furrows to the inch that divaricated light into a rainbow of spectral components and revealed much about the nature of the light's source.

Observed Dr. Kenner: "Throughout the symposium, before and after each day's session, a steady trickle of delegates managed to locate Room 30 in the basement of Rowland Hall, where Rowland's engine, recalled from decades of retirement, was suavely ruling one more grating as in the old days, stroke after deliberate stroke. The fragment of moon rock on display nearby rated a Pinkerton guard, but more people lingered longer before the ruling engine." He continued, "The ruling engine won't elucidate a golden age of physics.... Still, it embodies some quality which our longing for a golden age might wish to recapture. On the Shriver steps in a drizzle between conference papers, Dean George E. Owen was explicit about what one might wish to recapture. 'The Golden Age,' he pronounced, 'was when a man could make his own apparatus. And lift it.'"

No fewer than six Nobelists took part in the symposium, including physicist I.I. Rabi and laser inventor Charles Townes. Harvard's Edward Purcell discussed Rowland's famous experiment that showed that moving electrified bodies produce magnetic fields. The symposium extended over three days and ended with a strictly non-theoretical presentation by Edwin H. Land, chairman and research director of the Polaroid Corporation. Aided by a trailer-load of apparatus— and optical filters that made his packed Shriver Hall audience appear to be watching a 3-D movie—Land staged a dazzling display of modern optical pyrotechnics in the best lecture-room-spectacle tradition of Wood. Rowland, as Dr. Kenner noted, probably wouldn't have liked it.

* * *

The Rowland-Wood Symposium was a good example of the quality, significance, and enthusiastic response that was characteristic of the others. A typical symposium did not exist, for they were as varied as the individual participants and the wide-ranging subject matter they treated. Only a few others enjoyed the solo-spotlight luxury of Rowland-Wood, however, since as many events as possible were scheduled within the week in February 1976 that marked the exact centennial date—celebrated since the founding on February 22 as Commemoration Day.

Shortly before and during that week, a blizzard of local publicity was joined by news and editorial comment in such national publications as *The New York Times, The Washington Star, World* magazine, and the *Chronicle of Higher Education.* Commented the *Johns Hopkins Magazine:* "The Commemoration approached a three-ring atmosphere (as much as an intensely academic occasion ever could); it was not physically possible to attend even half the Commemoration events."

Consider Friday, February 20. At the School of Advanced International Studies in Washington, discussion of relations between more developed and less developed countries was under way among SAIS professors, the Jamaican ambassador to the United Nations, and a former member of the Allende cabinet in Chile. Twenty miles north on Maryland Route 29 at the Applied Physics Laboratory, a symposium on cosmology featured talks by Hannes Alfven, a Nobel laureate of the Royal Institute of Technology in Stockholm; S.I. Rasool, a planetary atmospheres expert with NASA; and W. Ian Axford, director of Germany's Max Planck Institute.

In East Baltimore at a symposium on international health at the School of Hygiene and Public Health, Rockefeller Foundation President John Knowles was contending that the next major advances in health care would stem not so much from improved technology as from changes in nutrition and individual lifestyles.

At Homewood, Linus Pauling and James D. Watson, both Nobelists (Pauling twice), spoke at a symposium on the impact of science on society. Also at Homewood that day took place a Humanities Center symposium, "The Responsibilities of the Critic," with noted Canadian literary critic Northrop Frye. James S. Coleman, who, while chairman of the University's Department of Social Relations in 1966 had written the famous report that became the basis of many school desegregation efforts, talked about controversial new directions in social policy research at a symposium named in honor of Dean Emeritus of Engineering Sciences Robert H.

Roy. And at an Evening College symposium, S.I. Hayakawa, president emeritus of San Francisco State University, spoke of the "revolution" in continuing college training for adults.

At 8:15 that evening in Baltimore's venerable Lyric Theater, the centennial ode received its first performance at a concert by the Baltimore Symphony Orchestra. Titled "A Song of Celebration" and written by poet John Hollander, the ode was set to music by the distinguished composer Hugo Weisgall, who received his doctorate from Johns Hopkins in 1940.

* * *

The first highlight of the following day—Saturday—was a symposium titled "The American University: The Second Hundred Years." Led by President Muller, panelists were Rev.

One of the most colorful figures in American science in the first half of the 20th century was Robert Williams Wood, professor of experimental physics. His work, which carried on the tradition of research in physical optics begun by Henry A. Rowland, was recognized at a symposium during the University's centennial celebration in 1976.

Theodore Hesbergh, president of Notre Dame; David E. Rogers, president of the Robert Wood Johnson Foundation and former dean of the Hopkins School of Medicine; Marcus Raskin, co-director of the Institute for Policy Studies; Congressman John Brademas, a member of the House Education and Labor Committee; and Hedley Donovan, editor-in-chief of Time, Inc. Much of the discussion centered around what was a proper role for universities in perpetuating the values of modern society and in government policy-making. In summing up, Dr. Muller previewed some of the ideas he would express more fully later in the day.

That occasion was the centennial banquet, an elegant affair at the Baltimore Hilton that drew 770 people in formal dress to dine on filet mignon and hear the president's major address of Commemoration week. After announcing that Hopkins Hundreds had thus far yielded $92,581,599 and proudly pronouncing complete success within reach, Dr. Muller spoke optimistically about the future of Johns Hopkins and universities in general. Quoting from President Gilman's inaugural speech in 1876, Dr. Muller singled out two short sentences which he saw as crystallizing the problem facing Johns Hopkins as it began its second century. Gilman had said: "Universities easily fall into ruts. Almost every epoch requires a fresh start."

Dr. Muller said that one effort Johns Hopkins was making toward a "fresh start" was in the reintegration of knowledge: "Even while intensive work continues in a multitude of highly specialized fields, and while new specialties are evolving, we are attempting to find ways to focus the various skills of specialists on problems that demand an integrated approach." As examples he cited the rewards of biomedical engineering research, the comprehensive approach being taken by the new Hopkins cancer center, foreign area programs at the School of Advanced International Studies, urban research by the Center for Metropolitan Planning and Research, and a new Atlantic History and Culture Program, among others.

Then he spoke of two other momentous changes which he believed were in sight. One was a major expansion of the concept of "life-long learning"—at Hopkins building upon the tradition of adult and continuing education pioneered by the Evening College. The second, he said, would stem from the enormous advances being made in communications and information technology. "On the basis of these two related new departures," he said, "I predict the onset of a mighty revolution in the university. I foresee the university transformed into a life-long learning center capable of training individuals on an individual basis anywhere on the globe—perhaps, before our second century ends, anywhere in the universe."

* * *

On Sunday, the focus of activity was once again the Lyric Theater where, just a few blocks from the site of President Gilman's inauguration exactly a century before, the University held its Centennial Commemoration Day Convocation.

As an orchestra played the academic processional, Hopkins faculty, trustees, and administrators in full academic regalia marched down the aisles to a stage wreathed in greens. With President Muller were the two living ex-presidents of the University, Milton S. Eisenhower and Lincoln Gordon. Joining them were the presidents of 53 other colleges and universities, ten of whom were Hopkins alumni. Trustees' chairman Robert D.H. Harvey opened the proceedings with the same words spoken 100 years before by Reverdy Johnson Jr. in opening the Gilman inaugural: "Our gathering here today is one of no ordinary interest." Following Mr. Harvey's remarks, Provost Harry Woolf presented the day's first honorary degree to Tito Carnacini, rector of the University of Bologna, which, Dr. Woolf said, had stood *in loco parentis* to the entire university system of the Western world.

The awarding of the second honorary degree—to Princess Ashraf Pahlavi of Iran—was interrupted by a small group of hecklers in the audience who were protesting political repression in Iran. The degree had been intended to recognize collaboration between Johns Hopkins and the College of Health Services in Tehran in the training of health professionals to serve the rural population of Iran. The controversy surrounding the award, however, later prompted Dr. Muller to call for policy guidelines for the making of such bestowals in the future. The third honorary degree went to Lord Eric Ashby, for many years master of Clare College at Cambridge University and an international figure in higher education.

* * *

This has been but a sampling of the flavor and richness of major centennial events. There were many other dimensions to the celebration. In connection with the observance, Johns Hopkins was host for the 1976 annual meeting of the Council of Learned Societies. Then there was the ubiquitous centennial symbol, rendered both as a logotype and as a clear plastic polyhedron in which was embedded a marble-size sphere consisting of a single crystal of aluminum—the crystals were produced by a process developed by Robert B. Pond, professor of materials science.

And could such a celebration be complete without a picnic? There was one, a party for all within the University community and their families on a warm Saturday afternoon in late April on the Wyman Quadrangle. Ten-cent beer and corn-on-the-cob supplemented the hot dog and hamburger menu staples, and there were baseball games and frisbees to help work off the extra calories.

"This has been a wonderful and eventful year to be associated with the Johns Hopkins Institutions," wrote Dr. Muller in his letter to alumni, parents, and friends of June 1976. "That joyful spirit was fully captured on May 15 at the Centennial Ball, the most gala event in the University's history. A volunteer committee chaired by Merle (Mrs. Owen) Phillips sponsored and arranged this extraordinarily happy event, attended by nearly 2,000 of us who danced to three bands in two huge tents on the Keyser and Wyman quadrangles, and which as a benefit also produced nearly $20,000 for undergraduate student aid."

At a press conference on Thursday, May 20, the day before the centennial commencement, Hopkins Hundreds national chairman Alonzo G. Decker Jr. formally reported that the campaign had not only met its goal on schedule but exceeded the $100 million target by nearly $9 million. Reported the *Johns Hopkins Journal*: "Thus concluded the most ambitious fund drive in the history of the Johns Hopkins Institutions, which was one of only 16 campaigns in the history of American higher education to raise more than $100 million." Mr. Decker noted that the goal was achieved in competition with the worst recession in the nation's recent history, and said these results spoke well for the future of privately supported institutions throughout the United States.

Except for two other events, the May 21 commencement brought the centennial observance and the academic year to a close. On a stormy mid-summer afternoon two months later, German Chancellor Helmut Schmidt addressed a special convocation in front of Gilman Hall that symbolically reaffirmed the traditions that President Gilman had transplanted from universities in Germany to the United States. In September, a commemorative lecture featured an address by Nobel laureate Sir Andrew Fielding Huxley, whose grandfather, Thomas Henry Huxley, had spoken at the opening of classes at the University in 1876.

* * *

The year's events, particularly the success of the Hopkins Hundreds campaign, had one other major impact that was not immediately observable but which became apparent before the decade ended. The late 1960s and early 1970s had been unhappy times for many universities in America. Anger and discontent over the protracted war in Vietnam, incredible financial pressures exerted on colleges and universities by double-digit inflation, an anti-intellectualism fad, and other factors had maligned the perception of higher education by large numbers of Americans and eroded the self-esteem of many within the academic community.

At Johns Hopkins, the procession of centennial events gave rise to a distinctly new spirit that was felt throughout the institution and which spread to alumni and other outside supporters as well. As one administrator put it: "The preoccupation with negative things suddenly disappeared, and people began to feel good about the place again."

A new sense of pride was badly needed. The centennial observance went a long way toward turning the "fresh starts" called for by Dr. Muller into real and viable possibilities.

Back in the black

There would have been no fresh starts—indeed, it would hardly have been possible even to carry on the University's business as before—had it not been for a restoration of financial stability. The story of how Johns Hopkins went from a succession of annual deficits that peaked at an alarming $4.2 million in 1971 and returned to fiscal good health in less than a decade is not just the story of a successful Hopkins Hundreds campaign, although it played an important part. General belt-tightening, administrative streamlining, and improved financial management were also major contributors.

The fact that this dramatic turnaround was accomplished during the 1970s makes it all the more impressive, for it was a trying time for all independent higher education institutions. The chief culprit was inflation, which hit double digits nationally but which chewed away at college and university budgets even more voraciously. Fuel and utility costs doubled; at Johns Hopkins, expenditures for plant operation and maintenance grew by a staggering 270 percent.

'... diminished reliance on federal money is clearly desirable. Planning under the present arrangement is extraordinarily difficult.'

Robert C. Bowie

In 1974, President Muller pegged the inflation rate for the University as a whole at 25 percent, more than twice the national average. He noted in his annual report that Hopkins could not practice economies of scale to any great extent, since that would involve admitting substantially larger numbers of students with an accompanying huge investment in additional faculty and physical facilities. "Unlike private business," he added, "the University cannot reduce costs substantially through automation. Education is labor-intensive—few of the important tasks that constitute the academic enterprise can be done by machine."

On top of these difficulties was piled the fact that Johns

Hopkins, like most research-oriented universities, was heavily reliant on the federal government for research support. While acknowledging this dependence on government money, President Muller declared: "The fact is that Johns Hopkins as it is today could not long survive without those funds, nor could any of the nation's private institutions where research is a major component of the academic venture. One problem is that in the United States, government policy for the funding of both research and training at institutions of higher learning has been left to blow with the political winds and is determined more by relatively short-term needs than by a steady development strategy."

Commenting on this problem in the financial report of the University for 1981-1982, Vice President for Finance and Treasurer Robert C. Bowie said: "With approximately half of its operating funds coming from various federal sources, Johns Hopkins is vulnerable to the vagaries of the annual appropriations process in Washington to the extent that a diminished reliance on federal money is clearly desirable. Planning under the present arrangement is extraordinarily difficult. Research projects of long standing can be extinguished overnight by a change in administration policy or Congressional attitude." As the decade of the 1980s reached midpoint, this problem had still not been resolved.

* * *

In spite of these impediments, the return to an era of balanced budgets was accomplished. It had been a primary concern of Dr. Eisenhower when he resumed the presidency in 1971, and President Muller not only continued his predecessor's cost-shaving initiatives but added his own, limiting faculty growth, further trimming administrative overlap, and leaving a number of staff vacancies temporarily unfilled. For the 1973-1974 academic year he was able to present—and the trustees gratefully approved—a balanced budget of $104.8 million. It was threatened for a time by the oil embargo and ensuing energy crisis, but survived, aided by increased alumni support and by a new formula for aid to private colleges and universities from the State of Maryland that included graduate degrees for the first time.

Once the institution was in the black, Dr. Muller vigorously pressed an effort to remain there, but no year passed when it was not a wrenching struggle. In addition to continuing high inflation through the 1970s, there were adverse changes in the revenue picture. Some large private foundations which had contributed generously to education in the preceding two decades began turning their priorities toward helping solve pressing national social problems. Government funding for research under both Democratic and Republican administrations was sharply curtailed. What government funding that did win approval was often accompanied by new conditions of accountability that made the hiring of additional administrative personnel necessary. There were large increases in employer contributions to the Social Security tax, and with some 10,000 people on its payrolls, the University was hard hit.

But balanced budgets continued to be the rule at Hopkins, and except for occasional short-term deficits in one division or another, there was nothing that approached the severe, institution-wide deficit picture of 1970 and 1971. Budgets were balanced, but salary increases lagged behind the rate of general inflation and there was little in the way of additional funding for student aid and library acquisitions. And there was one major casualty—the School of Health Services.

While the School had received generous backing from private sources at the outset, substantial federal support that had seemed assured during the planning stage was not forthcoming. When private support was exhausted, deficits mounted rapidly, and no way could be seen to operate the School in the black over the long run. Wrote trustees' chairman Robert D.H. Harvey in his insightful assessment of the first ten years of Dr. Muller's presidency: "With great regret and reluctance President Muller recommended, and the Trustees concurred, that the School be closed at the end of 1978. It had been a worthy undertaking requiring courage both at its inception and at its demise. The establishment of a first-rate program in nursing education remains as a goal for the University administration."

There were many factors in the University's ability to limit such catastrophes and to proceed along the difficult course toward fiscal vitality. Enough flexibility was inherent in the academic structure to permit cuts in some less promising fields and expansion in some areas of traditional strength and new promise. As mentioned, the Hopkins Hundreds campaign not only produced an emotional lift but provided funding for additional professorships throughout the institution. Other key factors included:

• Alumni Support—Considering its small size and translating that into a relatively small number of wealthy alumni, Johns Hopkins throughout the 1970s markedly improved its success in winning financial support from this sector. The alumni contribution to the $109 million raised through the Hopkins Hundreds was an impressive $41.1 million. At the same time, the regular annual alumni campaign, first known as the Roll Call and later the Annual Fund, continued to grow in importance. Gifts exceeded $2 million for the first time in the drive's 26-year history in 1972, and the $2 million mark was surpassed through the Hopkins Hundreds years. Annual Giving exceeded $3 million in 1978, $4 million in 1981, and in 1984 it produced $5.6 million. Although relatively small when compared with the University's total budget—$650 million for 1984-1985—these amounts were often just enough to make the difference between deficits and operating in the black.

• Other Private Giving—Despite several periods of sharp national economic downturn, a traditional dampening factor in philanthropy, Hopkins continued to attract substantial private gifts. A notable example was a 1976 bequest of $5.5 million from former trustee John Lee Pratt. This bequest, added to earlier gifts, made Mr. Pratt the University's greatest single benefactor to that time.

Overall, between 1978 and 1983, private giving to the University rose from $28.4 million to $41.0 million. Also during that time, the University fund-raising operation was strengthened. What had been known as the Johns Hopkins Fund became, in 1980, the Office of Development headed by a newly created vice presidency, the first incumbent being Robert J. Haley. In 1981, a Trustee Development Committee was established as a permanent committee of the boards of the University and Hospital to provide advice in all phases of

Evergreen House, an elegant mid-19th century mansion near Homewood, was given to the University in 1942 by John Work Garrett. It contains a library of more than 75,000 rare books, as well as unique collections of Japanese art, Chinese ceramics, and post-impressionist paintings.

development activity. Also in that year, the fund-raising staffs of the School of Medicine and Hospital were merged and renamed the Fund for Johns Hopkins Medicine.

• Endowment Income—A vital underpinning of the fiscal soundness that Johns Hopkins achieved following the near-disastrous early 1970s was the income from its invested endowment. Between 1972 and 1984, the endowment portfolio grew from $182 million to $326 million. Income from this source fluctuated slightly, depending on the performance of the major financial markets, but progressed upward from $6.8 million in 1974 to $22.1 million in 1985, well ahead of the inflation rate for the period.

• The Garrett Coins—In 1942, John Work Garrett, wealthy Baltimorean and University trustee, died and bequeathed to Johns Hopkins his magnificent North Charles Street residence, Evergreen, as well as one of the world's most valuable coin collections. For years, the coins remained locked in a vault at Evergreen, except for occasional small displays, attracting little public or scholarly attention. President Muller, concerned about problems of security, insurance costs, and the inability of the University to display the collection properly, recommended that the coins be sold. The trustees concurred, and at four auctions in New York and Los Angeles between 1979 and 1981, the collection brought record prices in the numismatic market. From the sales, the University realized a sum that exceeded all hopes—$21.4 million—which was added to the endowment of the School of Arts and Sciences. There were some who criticized the selling of the coins, but President Muller and the trustees believed the time was right to convert this substantial non-revenue-producing asset into badly needed endowment that would otherwise have taken years of intensive fund-raising to produce.

• Tuition—As the only component of its revenue that the University could control directly, tuition increases became a necessary consequence of inflation. Between 1970 and 1980, tuition at the Homewood divisions rose from $2,250 to $5,075 a year. In expressing his regret at the increases, President Muller noted that tuition at Hopkins was rising at a slower rate than at many peer institutions and that in terms of constant dollars discounted for inflation, the tuition rate remained almost level. He also noted that as tuition increased, so did student financial aid—by 230 percent between 1973 and 1983. During that time, about 70 percent of the University's undergraduates and 90 percent of its graduate students were receiving some form of financial assistance. In an effort to ease the monetary burden of undergraduate education, Hopkins in 1984 established a tuition stabilization program whereby four years of tuition could be prepaid based on the rate for the student's entering year, thereby avoiding the impact of future increases.

By 1985, tuition for the Homewood divisions had risen to $9,400 a year. This did represent an increase above the general inflation rate, which slowed during the early 1980s, but was necessary because of a massive construction and renovation program undertaken by the University starting in the late 1970s. It was felt that students, as beneficiaries of the improved facilities, should bear a small portion of their costs.

One of President Muller's deepest concerns about the expense of university education surfaced in 1981 and again in 1985 when the Reagan administration proposed drastic cuts in the federal student assistance program, the impact of which would have been felt most severely among middle-income families. In the *Johns Hopkins Gazette* of February 19, 1985, Dr. Muller wrote: "One of the grave consequences of severely cutting back aid is that private institutions—which account for some 20 percent of all undergraduate students—may again become accessible only to children of the upper and lowest income families. This would be a damaging and unhealthy turn in American education and would deprive a great many deserving students of the kind and quality of education they want and deserve."

• Sponsored Research—A research-oriented university depends heavily on the ability of its scholars and scientists to attract outside funding for their individual projects. Traditionally in the United States, the bulk of this support has come from the federal government, and Johns Hopkins was exceedingly successful in maintaining a high level of federal support even through the years when shriveling government appropriations for research hurt many institutions. Through the early 1980s, in fact, Hopkins ranked first among American research universities in total federal support when funds allocated to the Applied Physics Laboratory were included. Even excluding APL funds, notes the University's financial report for 1983-1984, Johns Hopkins was still among the top ten universities in research support, according to National Science Foundation figures.

• Indirect Cost Recovery—Along with the need to fund research in colleges and universities, the federal government recognized an obligation to reimburse institutions performing such research for the overhead expenses involved—space, utilities, janitorial costs, and the like. Until the mid-1970s, however, the overhead recovered by institutions did not reflect the true magnitude of those expenses. Johns Hopkins led an effort to correct this imbalance by identifying overhead costs more precisely and became a model for other institutions faced with the same problem. The importance of this change is shown by the fact that Hopkins' annual recoveries rose from $5.9 million in 1972 to $25.6 million in 1982.

• New Directions—In addition to efforts to improve the revenue flow from traditional sources, Johns Hopkins in the 1980s expanded its fund search into several areas that showed promise of future growth.

Money from the private corporate sector had long accounted for a small amount of sponsored research at the University, but in the face of the on-again, off-again attitude of the federal government toward the support of basic science, Hopkins sought to develop more private-sector funding. In 1983, the trustees approved a University-wide policy covering inventions developed with University support by Hopkins investigators. This was done not only to protect against possible loss of income but to enable the University to deal consistently with the growing number of corporate sponsors of research. Among the East Baltimore institutions, an organization known as the Dome Corporation was formed, primarily to explore the joint University-Hospital-corporate development of medical-related industries, such as pharmaceuticals.

Bricks and mortar

From the time when Gilman and his founding faculty occupied their modest quarters in downtown Baltimore, the bricks-and-mortar aspect of the operation always ranked below excellence in scholarship among the University's objectives. Yet, as the decade of the 1970s unfolded, it became increasingly clear, as it had in the first Eisenhower administration, that substantial investment in capital improvements was vital if the University were to remain competitive in attracting top researchers and students and in providing proper facilities for the conduct of modern science and scholarship.

A program of new construction and renovation of a magnitude unprecedented in the institution's history was undertaken—not for purposes of expansion but simply to provide existing departments, faculty, and students with new and better quarters, in some cases replacing facilities that had not been refurbished since they were built. By 1985, this program had raised the value of the University's physical plant to more than $383 million.

* * *

Spectacular changes were wrought on both Baltimore campuses, with the most dramatic impact occurring at the School of Medicine and Hospital where new construction completely altered the East Baltimore skyline. The first phase of a massive redevelopment program was approved in 1973, and, while it involved the Hospital most directly, it was closely related to the teaching and research activities of all the Johns Hopkins Medical Institutions.

In June 1974, ground was broken for the keystone of Phase One, a $15 million comprehensive cancer center that had been designated by the National Cancer Institute as a regional research and treatment center combining research laboratories and patient care facilities. Both the federal and state governments were instrumental in providing funds for the project, which was completed in 1976. Adjoining the center was a new eight-story patient care building that provided 180 inpatient beds. Phase One also included renovation of the Osler and Halsted buildings, a new administration building for the School of Medicine, and a sorely needed 720-space parking garage.

Another major component was a tower for the School of Medicine, which was named in honor of A. McGehee Harvey, emeritus professor, director of medicine, and physician-in-chief. This structure and the patient tower, which was named for Russell A. Nelson, emeritus president and trustee of the Hospital, marked a distinct departure from the century-old pavilion configuration at Hopkins. Newly constructed facilities featured horizontal layouts with medical, surgical, and other services occupying entire floors spanning as many as five connected buildings.

Phase Two commenced in 1978. Major elements included a new center for psychiatry and the neurosciences, a urology and nephrology institute, a new heart center, and a preclinical teaching building. To make way for these structures, the School of Medicine's original building, known familiarly as the Anatomy Building, was demolished. Another facility that filled a long-standing need was a new gymnasium and recreation center built near the medical students' residence hall. It was named in honor of a distinguished alumnus, Denton A. Cooley, who pledged $750,000 toward its construction through the Cooley Foundation.

A milestone was reached in the fall of 1981 when students of the Class of 1985 were the first to enter the new Preclinical Teaching Building. It arose on the same site where generations of medical students had undergone their arduous training since 1894. Bricks from the original structure were incorporated symbolically into the entrance of the new building, which included a 250-seat lecture hall, laboratory suites, multimedia study center, lounge, and dining area.

The fall of 1982 saw the dedication of three major buildings, as ten years and $150 million worth of modernization neared conclusion. The natural link between the Brady Urological Institute and the Department of Medicine's Nephrology Division was strengthened by new, shared facilities in a totally renovated Marburg Building. The new $42 million, nine-story neurosciences building was opened and named in honor of Adolf Meyer, founder of the Department of Psychiatry. The new Edward A. Maumenee Building was also opened, adding 40,000 square feet of research and outpatient space to the Wilmer Ophthalmological Institute. Dr. Maumenee was the Institute's former director.

While the Hospital's familiar dome remained as a point of reference, the East Baltimore campus continued to change at a blurring pace. New facilities included a heliport atop the Children's Center, a new Emergency Room, and an addition to the garage immediately south of the Hospital. In late 1983, the new Clayton Heart Center was dedicated, providing inpatient and outpatient facilities for pediatric and adult heart patients, as well as research and diagnostic laboratories. Viewed in one context, it was an era of noise, dust, inconven-

A new $21.7 million building for the Department of Biology was completed at Homewood in 1983. Named Seeley G. Mudd Hall for one of its benefactors, the four-level structure houses laboratories, classrooms, and offices. Other funding was provided by the National Cancer Institute.

ience, and some confusion, but out of it emerged a hospital and medical school complex with quarters and facilities second to none in the entire country.

At the School of Hygiene and Public Health, where there had been no major construction since the addition of wings to the main building in the late 1960s, plans were launched in 1985 for a $6.8 million program of construction and renovation. Of this sum, $2 million was contributed by the State of Maryland.

* * *

At Homewood during these years, a long list of needed physical facilities was headed by a new building for the Department of Biology, which had been squeezed into Mergenthaler Hall—built in 1941—with ever increasing discomfort, as the science expanded into molecular dimensions and grew in importance in such vital areas as cancer research and genetic engineering.

In addition to providing inadequate and poorly organized space, Mergenthaler suffered the woes of antiquated plumbing and electrical systems that broke down with dismaying regularity, often ruining delicate experiments and damaging costly apparatus. The go-ahead signal for new construction came in 1976, when the Seeley G. Mudd Fund of Los Angeles made a $1.5 million contribution to the project. A modified Georgian design was chosen for the four-level building, which was erected in three stages in a former park area north of Macaulay and Dunning Halls.

The first stage was completed in early 1979 just as the National Cancer Institute made a $2.6 million commitment to pay half the cost of the second stage. Work on the third and final stage was completed in early 1983, bringing the total cost of the imposing structure to $21.7 million. After years of frustration amid the confines of their Mergenthaler quarters, Hopkins biologists luxuriated in laboratories 60 feet deep with ceilings ten feet high, served by elaborate exhaust and 100 percent fresh air conditioning systems and a drainage system designed to minimize damage in case of flooding.

Dunning Park, a quiet haven that had occupied the site of the new building, was relocated to the wooded area between

Mudd Hall and the Athletic Center. Other changes included a new entrance to the campus at San Martin Drive near the Johns Hopkins Club. Robert G. Merrick, a 1917 alumnus and former University trustee, provided funds for a handsome, Georgian-style entrance gate, as he had previously for entrances at the southern edge of the campus and at the main entrance on Charles Street.

The next major project for Homewood was a milestone for two reasons: it provided a magnificent new home for the Department of Earth and Planetary Sciences, and it marked the first advance by the University across San Martin Drive—once the western boundary of the Homewood campus—into territory that had been Wyman Park. In fact, the land was originally part of a large tract that had been given to the University in 1902 by William Wyman. When Baltimore City began creating Wyman Park a few years later, the University donated 52 acres to help.

In 1960, President Eisenhower foresaw the University's eventual need to expand and asked the city to sell 70 acres just west of San Martin Drive. There was opposition from local residents, however, and the city agreed to sell only 30 acres. It was on part of this land that the new Earth and Planetary Sciences building, financed by a $4.7 million grant from the Olin Foundation, was built, providing the department with long-needed additional research and office space.

University construction crossed San Martin Drive a second time in 1983, when a new $9.5 million building was erected for the Space Telescope Science Institute. (The selection of Johns Hopkins as the Institute's home base will be discussed fully in a later section.) In the summer of 1985, with the encouragement of Mayor Schaefer, the University requested the Baltimore Board of Recreation and Parks to sell or lease to Johns Hopkins 35 acres of Wyman Park land still under city jurisdiction. The request was prompted by the interest of several research organizations in affiliating with the University and constructing facilities adjacent to the Space Telescope Science Institute. The University formulated a plan to develop a portion of the existing parkland, but the plan encountered opposition from residents of the area west and northwest of the park. In November, a special task force set up to study the problem recommended a compromise under which the University would convert land west of San Martin Drive then serving as athletic fields into building sites; new playing fields would be developed in existing parkland, thus preserving the open character of the area which nearby residents sought to maintain.

Another area of serious and long-standing concern at Homewood was the quality of student life. Living accommodations and food service on the campus had fallen below the standards offered by many peer institutions, and, in 1981, the University announced a major effort to upgrade those services.

A $24 million Student Amenities Program was implemented which called for complete renovation of the Alumni Memorial Residences, construction of two new dormitories to provide additional on-campus housing, and improvement of food service and recreation facilities. The last phase added a 400-seat dining room and new space for such student activities as social and cultural functions, a reading room, and a television lounge. All of the new facilities were air-conditioned, opening the way for increased use of the campus during the summer months. University-owned off-campus housing, which served about 40 percent of the graduate student population at Homewood in the early 1980s, was also targeted for refurbishing.

Homewood Field—that time-honored arena where Hopkins lacrosse squads and stars of other collegiate sports displayed their prowess over the years—was extensively renovated in 1981. Because of the difficulty and expense of maintaining grass year-round in the Baltimore climate, an artificial playing surface was installed, making possible much more extensive use of the field by Hopkins teams and those of other schools. A new lighting system was also installed, as was an all-season track. These improvements were completed in time to make Homewood a first-class site for the 1982 World Lacrosse Games that brought top teams from the United States, Canada, Great Britain, and Australia to compete in this olympics of lacrosse.

Homewood House, the mansion that gave the campus its name and set its architectural tone for years, underwent a renovation starting in 1984. Built in 1801 at the then-staggering cost of $40,000, the house had served a variety of purposes, including a faculty club and offices for the deans and president. A 1973 endowment by Mr. Merrick made possible a major restoration of the structure, which was designated a National Historic Landmark in 1976. The endowment also enabled the University to initiate plans to furnish the building with period antiques and open it as a public museum. Further generosity by Mr. Merrick made possible the renovation of another of the Carroll estate's original buildings known as The Barn, which had served since 1942 as the home of Theater Hopkins.

* * *

At the Applied Physics Laboratory, construction in the early 1980s was highlighted by completion of a new conference and education center. Named in honor of former director and chief scientist Alexander Kossiakoff, the center provided new classrooms for the growing graduate engineering programs conducted at APL, as well as a 500-seat auditorium and dining facilities. In 1984, the R.B. Kershner Space Systems Integration and Test Facility was dedicated in honor of the man who had headed space research at APL for more than two decades. The $8 million structure provided new laboratory space and test equipment designed to enhance the Laboratory's capabilities in satellite development.

In 1984, the School of Continuing Studies opened spacious new quarters for its growing operation in Columbia, Maryland. Another branch of the University that felt growing pains during this period was the School of Advanced International Studies. In late 1985, an additional building a block from the existing SAIS building was acquired, which was expected to meet the School's space needs for the foreseeable future.

* * *

In November 1985, the University set the stage for another major round of construction and renovation by acquiring $181 million through bonds issued by the Maryland Health and Higher Education Facilities Authority. It was the largest issue ever undertaken by Johns Hopkins or approved by the

Authority and was designed to finance projects University wide through the 1980s. Among the projects planned were renovation of Gilman, Ames, and Remsen Halls and a new building for the Department of Physics and Astronomy at Homewood, a new research building for the Department of Medicine in East Baltimore, and an additional research and office building for the Space Telescope Science Institute.

Signposts

Academic developments at Johns Hopkins in the years following 1976 were as momentous in terms of the University's future course as the dramatically improved physical plant. These developments can best be placed in perspective if the centennial dinner address of President Muller is recalled. At that time, after five years at the helm of the Hopkins institutions, he put forth three themes that impressed him as being strong determinants of the University's future.

First he spoke of the "reintegration of knowledge." This was really an extension of the concept of cohesion that has been used to characterize the Eisenhower presidency. Reintegration of knowledge meant the application of whatever distinct and usually separate disciplines it took to focus on a given problem or series of problems. Interdisciplinary activity, which both satisfied the philosophical need for coherence and proved a highly productive technique in research scholarship, was an old Hopkins hallmark that Dr. Muller saw as becoming even more important under a new set of circumstances and conditions.

Examples of this kind of activity abound in the University's postcentennial history. The most recent—and one of the most clearly illustrative—surfaced in 1984, when consideration was begun of the establishment at Johns Hopkins of a major new research unit to study problems arising from interactions between the human mind and brain. President Muller and Provost Richard P. Longaker formed a University task force in response to strong faculty interest in the interdisciplinary study of cognitive science and neuroscience. The 70-member group represented no fewer than eight of the University's divisions and embraced the fields of biophysics, biology, physiology, neuroscience, linguistics, philosophy, psychology, psychiatry, computer science, electrical engineering, and biomedical engineering.

In 1985, visiting consultants in these fields began a series of meetings with members of the University group to help refine the concept of the new unit and plan for its form and substance. Three broad areas of investigation emerged as the basis for collaborative research projects: *neuroscience* (the brain); *cognitive science* (the mind); and *artificial intelligence* as a vital bridge between the two. Out of these meetings grew an awareness of a rare opportunity for Johns Hopkins to harness its extraordinary academic talent and clinical resources in a focused effort to advance understanding of the mind-brain interaction. At the same time, the University would be creating a new kind of interdisciplinary unit which—in the Hopkins tradition but with unprecedented sweep—transcended traditional departmental precincts and divisional barriers that still exist in many research universities.

* * *

The second basic idea advanced by Dr. Muller was the concept of "life-long learning." In an interview nine years later in 1985, he said the concept still applied, and with greater force than ever: "We've got to acknowledge that we cannot turn out a finished product at any level. We can bring people to the state of the art, but we know that the state of the art is going to change within a decade, possibly less. We have to furnish—at a professional and at a general level— that continued learning assistance that will keep people in tune, either with their own field or a new field as their professional lives evolve."

Dr. Muller's third point, the impact of the revolution in information technology, brought changes in the way the University went about its business that even the most visionary prophet of the electronic age would have had difficulty forecasting in 1976. The most striking example: less than a decade later, Hopkins was building its own earth satellite station to make possible direct communication with information resources around the world.

Along with these three themes a fourth emerged with astonishing strength in the early 1980s. From its founding, Johns Hopkins had displayed an international character, but this aspect flourished as advances in communication permitted ever-widening extension of the University's influence on the world of ideas.

In the sections that follow, it will be evident that these

themes underlay many of the important activities and changes that took place within the various divisions of the University in the years after 1976.

Gilman Hall, a stately Georgian-style structure and the first major building completed at Homewood, has provided classrooms, library facilities, and office space for Hopkins humanities departments since it opened in 1915.

Lifestream disciplines

Woodrow Wilson once described the kind of study for which Johns Hopkins stood as that "which has its face forward to the future and whose object is the extension of the realm of knowledge." By encouraging that kind of study, Wilson continued, "it has been made evident that knowledge lives; that it is a part of the power of achievement, fit to serve the nation in the present and the future."

Those observations captured well not only the essence of Gilman's unique venture in American higher education, but the goal of that cluster of disciplines which evolved and exists today in colleges and universities under the rubric of "arts and sciences." As it was in Wilson's day, arts and sciences in the years following the University's centennial were still the lifestream of Johns Hopkins, still healthy and robust despite global changes both within the constituent fields and in the environment in which they existed.

Two aspects of the modern history of arts and sciences at Johns Hopkins will be examined as illustrative of the whole picture: the importance of the broad-based, interdisciplinary approach that is a Hopkins-fostered tradition in the United States, and the emergence in the early 1980s of the University as a world center for research in astronomy.

Some of the changes that took place during the period had to do with the basic role of arts and sciences in the modern

'... this has always been a volatile place, but in a positive way. Whenever something looks as if it's breaking down or splintering or fragmenting, it has always meant the coming of something new.'

Harry Sieber

American research university, a role which was widely acknowledged in the 1970s to be declining. The growth in size and strength among the professional faculties in many institutions eroded the unifying function that a faculty of arts and

A new home for the Department of Earth and Planetary Sciences was provided by Olin Hall, which opened at Homewood in 1982. It was named in recognition of a $4.85 million grant from the Olin Foundation, Inc.

sciences had traditionally provided. Increasing early specialization among students tended to fragment arts and sciences disciplines. And the arts and sciences—which were historically heavily dependent on general institutional funds—were more vulnerable to financial pressures upon universities than divisions which related more directly to applied professions and which were able to attract specialized support on that basis.

Among the arts and sciences themselves, the area most seriously affected by developments in the 1970s was the humanities. Colleges and universities nationally were being taken to task by education experts for allowing the humanities to be swallowed up by specialized training. The culmination was a November 1984 indictment by the National Endowment for the Humanities which said American college students were being "shortchanged" in the humanities and were graduating without even the most rudimentary knowledge of the history, literature, art, and philosophical foundations of the nation.

Of all the generalizations that can be made about Hopkins, one of the truest is undoubtedly that the institution more often than not runs counter to national trends. Such was clearly the case with respect to arts and sciences and particularly the humanities in the postcentennial period. One of the most important evolutionary developments at the University during this time was a dramatic strengthening in the humanities. It took place in spite of the financial pressures on the arts and sciences, the interest among undergraduates to specialize early, and declining financial support for graduate students in this area. Hopkins was by no means immune to those pressures, but these are among the things that were accomplished:

• Between 1975 and 1984, there were 15 new senior faculty appointments among the nine departments in the humanities and four appointments at the associate professor level. Considering the small size of Hopkins' departments, the addition of even one person sometimes represented a quantum jump in depth and teaching capacity.

• In 1982, new rankings of doctoral programs among American universities by the Conference Board of Associated

Research Councils placed the Johns Hopkins departments of English, History, and History of Art among the top ten, even when compared with departments as much as five times larger in other institutions.

• Despite a nationwide decline in the number of graduate students in the humanities brought on by reductions in federal and foundation support and a growing awareness that there was not an infinitely expanding market for people with graduate research degrees, Hopkins continued very much in the business of training research scholars. Some of these men and women brought financial support with them in the form of prestigious at-large grants, and few on leaving had difficulty finding teaching and research jobs in their fields.

• Major new funding was secured for development of the humanities at the University, including a $900,000 challenge grant from the National Endowment for the Humanities and grants totaling $1.5 million from the Andrew W. Mellon Foundation.

• A new dimension of opportunities for Hopkins students in the humanities was created with the affiliation in 1977 between the University and the Peabody Institute, one of the nation's most renowned conservatories of music.

* * *

A search for reasons why developments like these were able to take place at Hopkins leads back to the familiar concepts of cohesion, the reintegration of knowledge, and interdisciplinarity. They were factors in the strengthening of the humanities perhaps more so than many other areas, and they enhanced the University's appeal in the recruitment of new funds, new faculty, and high caliber undergraduate and graduate students.

The traditional permeability of departmental walls at the University was nowhere better exemplified than in the work of the Humanities Center, which served as a catalyst in the interplay and cross-communication that made ten administratively autonomous departments often function as a whole. One of the center's noteworthy achievements was establishment in the late 1970s of an undergraduate Honors Program in Humanistic Studies. It was coordinated by a board of tutors representing different departments and permitted exceptionally well-qualified students to earn B.A and M.A. degrees concurrently in areas of comparative literature, intellectual history, or period studies in several of the arts.

In an article on the Humanities Center in the Spring 1983 issue of the *Johns Hopkins Journal,* director Michael Fried, who came to the University from Harvard in 1975, said: "One of the virtues of an operation like the Humanities Center is that it enables us to do things that individual departments might not feel free to do or be able to do as easily. We're supposed to come up with ideas that cut across departments and to explore unorthodox possibilities. Hopkins is committed to doing those sorts of things and it's very helpful to have someplace where this effort gets focused. My feeling about the Humanities Center is that it has such a natural place at Hopkins that if the center ceased to exist next week, it would get re-invented within a month, because in a way it makes explicit what Hopkins is all about."

* * *

The small relative size of Johns Hopkins has often been cited as a facilitator of intellectual movement and exchange between disciplines. An article on the University in the Summer 1976 issue of *World* magazine said: "The smallness of Hopkins ... has helped create a place of great scholastic flexibility, a place that has possibly the maximum potential for interaction among disciplines, where administrative decisions can be made without going through echelons of bureaucratic fat, where certain things can be done academically that would be unthinkable in a larger institution, where everyone on a given campus can almost literally know everyone else."

Hopkins was small, but, as noted earlier, size never stopped many of its departments from earning reputations comparable with those of much larger institutions. The School of Arts and Sciences in the 1984-1985 school year consisted of 23 academic departments. Faculty numbered 300. There were 1,820 undergraduates and 786 graduate students. The only significant change in the enrollment pattern was a decline during the period in the number of graduate students in some areas. In undergraduate enrollment, Johns Hopkins was unaffected by a national decline in the number of college-age men and women that began to be felt by many institutions in the early 1980s. Applicants to Hopkins reached record levels (nearly 5,000 a year to fill 600 freshman class openings) and, even more important, so did their academic qualifications. In 1982-1983, for example, the mean Scholastic Aptitude Test score for Hopkins freshmen was 1,280 (verbal and mathematical), as compared with the national average of 888. Typically, 75 percent or more had graduated in the top tenth of their high school classes.

Women during the early 1980s became completely integrated into all phases of undergraduate life and by 1985 accounted for about 40 percent of the student body.

* * *

The attractiveness of Hopkins to both graduate and undergraduate students was unquestionably enhanced by the many options for interdisciplinary study, which were widely available in other areas besides the humanities. Expanding capabilities to study organic matter at the molecular level led to new alliances among biology, chemistry, and biophysics in basic cancer research at Homewood. The wedding of computer science and electrical engineering was formally recognized in a new departmental name. The Department of Physics became the Department of Physics and Astronomy. Social Relations became Sociology.

Within the humanities, philosophy saw not only a rebirth of interest in its history but a growing commitment to the philosophy of science and new concern in such "applied" areas as medical ethics and death. Another old Hopkins stronghold, Near Eastern Studies, was faltering but was dramatically resuscitated by a $1.25 million gift to endow a chair to memorialize William F. Albright. In literary studies, there was a surge of interest in rereadings of canonical German texts in philosophy and psychoanalysis from the viewpoint of contemporary currents in French and American criticism. The anthropologically oriented structuralist movement in literary theory—introduced to America via the Humanities Center in 1966—evolved in the 1970s into "deconstruction," which brought to bear on literary studies the analytical methods of Freud and other psychoanalysts and philosophers, and united the practitioners of those disciplines accordingly. One department that had been an intellectual monument at Hopkins from the earliest days, Romance Languages, split into a Department of French and a Department of Hispanic and Italian Studies.

Commenting on the breakup, the Winter 1984 *Johns Hopkins Journal* said: "Some observers of the Hopkins scene saw it as the end of an era." It noted the prominence achieved by the University in philology through Leo Spitzer and his successor, Anna Hatcher. Not all viewed the change with gloom, however. Professor of Spanish Harry Sieber, named to head the new Department of Hispanic and Italian Studies, saw the change as being in the mold of a Hopkins tradition that had repeatedly set the University apart in the field of American letters. "In my own time here, 16 years," Dr. Sieber said, "this has always been a volatile place, but in a positive way. Whenever something looks as if it's breaking down or splintering or fragmenting, it has always meant the coming of something new." He foresaw more interest in his own area as a result of growing national concern with Latin America and increasing cooperative academic efforts with the departments of History and Political Science and with the School of Advanced International Studies. "You can never legislate these kinds of things," Dr. Sieber added. "They simply develop with good chemistry, which is something Hopkins has provided so often in the past."

In another example of new combinations, History, Anthropology, and Sociology found much in common in area studies of Atlantic civilizations. This took form in 1972 in the Program in Atlantic History, Culture and Society, a cross-disciplinary examination of the linked pasts and common experiences of societies bordering the Atlantic basin. The program was the springboard for creation of the Department of Anthropology at Hopkins and for the addition of new faculty specialists in the Department of History. Research under the program did much to redefine and reformulate the way that social science research in that area of the world and other Third World nations was conducted and interpreted.

Another example of strongly interdisciplinary graduate study and research was the Johns Hopkins Center for Italian Studies. Located in a handsome Italian country house known as Villa Spelman in Florence, Italy, in the heartland of the ancient Etruscan-Roman civilization, the center has become both a focal point for programs on the Italian Renaissance in the departments of History and the History of Art, and a major intellectual presence in Italy as the setting for seminars given by experts in Italian history and culture.

* * *

Just as it had in graduate education, a clear need emerged during the 1970s and early 1980s for a broader scope in undergraduate training. The increasing early specialization sought by many students had been a concern at Hopkins for some time, and apart from programs to encourage premedical students to heighten their exposure to the humanities, the University attempted to facilitate interdisciplinary work among all undergraduates. Area major programs were developed to give students a solid grounding in any of five broad fields of learning: Humanistic Studies, including the literature, history, and philosophy of a particular age or region; Natural Sciences, which encompassed all the so-called hard sciences and some engineering specialties; Human Biology, primarily for premedical students and others interested in public health, behavioral sciences, or bioengineering; Quantitative Studies, for areas heavily dependent on mathematical skills; and Social and Behavioral Sciences, for those interested in such fields as law, urban studies, business and management, and political science. In each area, the scope was broader than that offered through traditional departmental majors—which were also available—without sacrificing depth and rigor.

One of the most popular undergraduate offerings in the early 1980s was an International Studies Program given through the Department of Political Science. Along with intensive work in specialized geographic areas, students who chose this major took courses in language, history, politics, economics, psychology, and social relations bearing on their fields of special interest.

Among several unique facilities that are part of the University is Villa Spelman, a 16th-century estate in Florence, Italy, now home of the Charles S. Singleton Center for Italian Studies. Its graduate programs in Renaissance studies and Italian art typify the inter-disciplinary approach to the humanities that has been characteristic of Johns Hopkins since its earliest days.

In addition to the national honor accorded to the Johns Hopkins departments of English, History, and History of Art, there was other evidence that the University's gains in the arts and sciences were being widely recognized. In 1979, *Change* magazine reported that since 1964, Johns Hopkins had moved from 21st to 15th place in the rankings of colleges and universities preferred by the most highly qualified applicants for undergraduate admission. There were many marks of individual recognition, including a $284,000 MacArthur Foundation Fellowship to Philip Curtin, Herbert Baxter Adams Professor of History; the election of biology professor Ru Chih Chow Huang to the Chinese Academy of Science, only the second woman to be so honored; the election of Biology Chairman William Harrington to the National Academy of Sciences; and a personal request to Dr. Muller from British Prime Minister Margaret Thatcher in 1980 to grant a leave of absence to Alan Walters, professor of political economy, so that he could serve as her personal economic adviser.

* * *

Research in the physical, biological, and social sciences at Homewood continued at a brisk pace in the 1980s, less restrained by financial considerations than the humanities but off the blank-check pace of the 1960s. Highlights included:

• Advances in the understanding of the molecular anomalies of hemoglobin in sickle cell anemia made by physiologist Warner Love through new techniques in X-ray crystallography.

• New insights from biologist Saul Roseman as to how, in the incredible process of cell differentiation by which a single cell grows into a complex organism, cells get signals from and recognize other cells that surround them.

• Experiments in the development of languages by which people communicate with computers by professor of psychology Alphonse Chapanis, which helped bring him the American Psychological Association's highest honor.

• A first step in developing a new theory of vulcanism by volcanologist Bruce Marsh, who formed a model of the subterranean cage in which volcanoes are born that made it possible to determine the amount of underlying magma.

• Contributions by biochemist Maurice Bessman to an

understanding of the mechanism of error-correcting enzymes in DNA replication and of factors that lead to high mutation rates in various organisms.

• One of the first scanning electron microscopes powerful enough to "see" an individual atom, developed by biophysicist Michael Beer and put to work deciphering the genetic message in DNA molecules.

• "Living light" or bioluminescence studies over a 30-year span by biologist Howard Seliger that led from fireflies to new knowledge of the metabolism of certain carcinogens and a non-destructive assay for their detection.

• Research by sociologist Alejandro Portes that discredited conventional views on immigration policies and signaled new scholarly concern with the economic problems and potentials of the country's new immigrants.

• Discovery by biologist Evangelos Moudrianakis of the molecular structure of a protein complex, called the histone octamer, that lay at the core of chromosomes and was believed to play a key role in the organization of genetic material and, indirectly, in the regulation of gene expression.

• Fundamental research in experimental high energy physics conducted at the world's largest accelerator laboratories by a Hopkins group led by Aihud Pevsner, Leon Madansky, and Chih Yung Chien.

• Discovery by biophysicist Shin Lin of a protein in human blood platelets that affected the machinery responsible for the ways in which both normal cells and cancer cells moved.

• Mapping of the structure of the DNA molecule by chemist Thomas D. Tullius, taking advantage of new sequencing techniques and the interaction between DNA and an antitumor drug, cysplatin.

• Development of a simple bacterial test by biologist Philip Hartman that was responsible for discovering carcinogenic properties in a widely used drug and in a fire retardant used in children's pajamas.

* * *

No stream of intellectual inquiry flowed more persistently through the course of Johns Hopkins science than astronomy. Usually associated with mountaintop observatories in clear-skied western states, astronomy in fact owed many of its spectacular 20th-century achievements to tools and techniques developed in cramped workrooms in the University's original Howard Street buildings and later in the laboratories of Rowland Hall. How appropriate, then, that Baltimore—specifically the Homewood campus as site of the Space Telescope Science Institute—should eventually become the focal point of astronomical research for the entire world.

The first player in this century-spanning drama was Henry A. Rowland; his diffraction gratings made possible the field of spectroscopy, which became the foundation of analytical work in modern physics as well as in astronomy. For years, Rowland was supplier to the world of precision diffraction gratings.

Simon Newcomb, one of the most famous American astronomers of the 19th century, became professor of mathematics and astronomy at Johns Hopkins in 1884. Also connected with the Naval Observatory in Washington, Newcomb was noted for originality in the mathematical treatment of astronomical data and for theoretical research on the motions of planetary moons. One of his small telescopes was proudly displayed at the Rowland-Wood exhibit during the centennial.

It was Wood who picked up the Rowland tradition at Hopkins when he joined the faculty in 1901, the year of Rowland's death. Wood further refined the ruling engine and produced diffraction gratings for some of the world's largest observatories, including the Mount Palomar facility in California that opened in 1939. Wood also did research on the use of absorption screens in astronomical photography.

One of Wood's contemporaries at Hopkins was A. Herman Pfund, an American pioneer in infrared spectrum investigations. Pfund perfected methods that were used half a century later in high altitude research on planetary atmospheres. One who did such studies in the 1950s was physicist John Strong, whose detectors, hoisted far above the southwestern desert by balloons, analyzed light from the planet Venus. Rockets replaced balloons in the 1960s for lofting instrumentation packages above the earth's atmosphere, and with substantial support from the National Aeronautics and Space

Administration, Hopkins scientists expanded their research to include stars and extremely distant quasar-like objects. Warren Moos obtained the first precise look at the ultraviolet spectrum of the solar system's nearest neighbor, Alpha Centauri. Physicist Paul Feldman and chemist John Doering designed experiments to study the aurora borealis and other phenomena using NASA rockets fired from Ft. Churchill, Canada, and White Sands, New Mexico. William Fastie developed highly precise instrumentation to make astronomical observations in the key ultraviolet range, and one of his spectrometers went to the moon aboard Apollo 17, where it yielded valuable insights into the composition of the thin lunar atmosphere.

New faculty in astrophysics strengthened the University's program in the early 1970s, but virtually all the work continued to be based on the precision spectroscopy pioneered

Johns Hopkins was chosen as host university for the National Aeronautics and Space Administration's Space Telescope Science Institute, which occupied this modern building in 1983. The facility was designed as headquarters for science operations of the Hubble Space Telescope.

by Rowland. Orbiting satellites joined rockets as instrument platforms—Richard Henry and Dr. Moos used NASA's Copernicus satellite in 1975 to study ultraviolet and X-radiation given off by "cool" stars, such as the sun. In 1977, a rocket team led by physicist Arthur F. Davidsen discovered atomic hydrogen in the ultraviolet spectrum of the quasar 3C273; among the implications: the universe may not be ever-expanding. It was a major contribution to modern cosmology.

Dr. Davidsen and his colleagues also studied planets and pulsars and, with the Applied Physics Laboratory, designed and built "HUT," the Hopkins Ultraviolet Telescope, to scan the skies from aboard NASA's Space Shuttle. This project produced Hopkins' first astronaut, astrophysicist Samuel T. Durrance, who was chosen as a Space Shuttle payload specialist to operate the telescope. At a press conference announcing his selection in 1984, Dr. Durrance was given a T-shirt emblazoned with the words: "HUT—Another Giant Step for Hopkins." Also that year, the Department of Physics changed its name to Physics and Astronomy.

Even its own man and hardware in space was not the biggest news in Hopkins astronomy in the 1980s. That was by any reckoning the selection by NASA in 1981 of the Homewood campus as the site for its Space Telescope Science Institute, which was expected to become the center of worldwide research in astronomy for decades to come. Riding an orbiting satellite 320 miles above the earth and its obscuring atmosphere, the Space Telescope would be able to see objects 50 times fainter than those visible from earth-based telescopes and ten times further into the universe—98 percent back, in fact, to the beginning of time. One key element in the Space Telescope's optical system was the same kind of diffraction grating that Rowland had developed a century before; another was a spectrograph invented by Wood.

It should be made clear that the Institute was not part of the University but is operated under contract to the National Aeronautics and Space Administration by a 15-member consortium, the Association of Universities for Research in Astronomy, Inc. Hopkins is a member of the consortium, and the Space Telescope itself is a joint undertaking of NASA and the European Space Agency. The Hopkins tradition of fundamental contributions to the science over the years was an important factor in the consortium's endorsement of the Homewood site, as were the University's willingness to construct and help finance the Institute's $9 million building and the proximity of the Goddard Space Flight Center in Greenbelt, Maryland, where the orbiting telescope's data would be received. The University and the Institute also established strong academic ties. Director Riccardo Giacconi holds a joint faculty appointment, and Hopkins astrophysicists assisted in the design and testing of key components for the telescope and expected to benefit enormously from the constant stream of visiting scientists who would use the Institute's unparalleled facilities.

The presence of the Space Telescope Science Institute afforded Johns Hopkins a unique opportunity to develop one of the world's leading programs in astrophysics and space science. Toward that end, in May 1985, Arts and Sciences Dean George W. Fisher announced plans to double the number of faculty in the field and develop a major new Center for Astrophysical Sciences on the campus near the Institute. Dr. Davidsen, named director of the new center, noted in a newspaper interview that other leading universities in the field were already seeking Hopkins' collaboration in new research ventures. "We are suddenly a major player in the action," he said, adding in a spirit of unabashed intramural competition: "To make Hopkins as well known for astrophysics as it is for medicine is my goal."

A new school for engineering

The recent history of engineering at Johns Hopkins is a clear example not only of the concept of reintegration of knowledge, but of the advantages afforded by the flexibility of divisional and departmental lines that has made interdisciplinary academic activity at the University a rule rather than an exception.

In the years following 1966, when the School of Engineering Science merged with the Faculty of Philosophy, programs in engineering were carried on primarily in three academic departments: Electrical Engineering, Mechanics and Materials Science, and Geography and Environmental Engineering. A small group of faculty with interests in operations research existed within the Department of Mathematical Sciences, and an interdivisional committee administered a program in bioengineering. Important research went forward, and students who graduated from these programs had no trouble finding jobs.

Overall, however, engineering at Hopkins went into a slow decline. Without the administrative buttress afforded by a separate school, engineering departments suffered more than many others during the financial crisis of the early 1970s. Crucial investments in new equipment were deferred, and buildings were not adequately maintained. The faculty, which had been close to 60 when the merger occurred, dropped to just above 40. To some outside observers, particularly alumni and potential private and corporate supporters, it appeared that Hopkins had abandoned engineering alto-

'A lot of people in industry had forgotten about us. We had to sell our commitment to having a first-rate engineering school. There was a period at first when a lot of people out there didn't believe it was anything but eyewash.'

V. David VandeLinde

gether. This, of course, was not the case, but the false perception became entrenched through the early 1970s.

* * *

Gradually, it became clear that Hopkins had made a mistake, and, in 1975, President Muller charged a blue-ribbon committee chaired by Lawrence R. Hafstad, retired vice president and research director for General Motors and a former University trustee, to review the role of the engineering sciences at the University. In its report in the fall of 1976, the committee acknowledged the record of accomplishment by the engineering departments since the merger, but said that the problem of identity loss had brought engineering science at Hopkins to a critical point:

"From the administrative point of view, the sense of discomfort seems to arise from the fact that, in the industrial world, Hopkins is considered to have lost all interest in practical engineering activities. Individual professors may be known and even acclaimed, but there is no 'School of Engineering' to attract students interested in working in industry. There is little incentive for industry to support an institution not sensitive to its needs for broadly trained leaders capable of managing major engineering projects."

The committee, which represented both the academic and industrial communities, felt strongly that Hopkins had the tradition behind it to create an academic "center of excellence" which could make a substantial contribution to engineering both nationally and in the Baltimore area. It considered a number of options, ranging from phasing out engineering altogether to the reestablishment of a School of Engineering that was independent of the division of Arts and Sciences. The latter course won the committee's unanimous endorsement as the option that held the greatest promise of placing Johns Hopkins once again in the forefront of engineering education in the United States.

"This school should be small," the committee's report said, "of high quality, and professionally oriented.... A relatively stable undergraduate curriculum will be required to ensure the broad technical base and versatility which a young graduate moving into industry is expected to have.

However, the emphasis should be on educating leaders for the engineering profession. For this a strong graduate program, also practice oriented, is absolutely essential. It is here that the talent available in the existing strong program in engineering sciences can make its greatest contribution and, at the same time, ensure its continued support."

The committee readily recognized the problem areas involved in carrying out its recommendation, such as financial and physical resources, faculty motivation, and administrative commitment. As it turned out, the faculty generally approved of the move, and President Muller led the commitment. The University trustees gave their approval, and planning and fund-raising went forward. In June 1979, Dr. Muller was able to announce that a new school of engineering would be formally opened in the fall, thanks in large measure to $5 million in new endowment secured for that purpose. Of this sum, $3 million came from the estate of former student and prominent Baltimore engineer and builder G.W.C. Whiting, for whom the new school was named. (In 1982, Mrs. Whiting gave another $1.5 million for an endowed professorship in civil engineering.) Soon thereafter, a young professor of electrical engineering, V. David VandeLinde, was named dean of engineering and given a mandate to rebuild the school.

* * *

The first step was to build a base from which credibility could be reestablished. When the School first opened, Dean VandeLinde said in the *Johns Hopkins Magazine* in February 1985, he had to work hard just to get people to acknowledge that Hopkins was in the engineering business. "A lot of people in industry had forgotten about us," he said. "We had to sell our commitment to having a first-rate engineering school. There was a period at first when a lot of people out there didn't believe it was anything but eyewash. You convince them not by talking a good story, but by showing them some accomplishments."

At the end of five years, the new School had more than a few accomplishments to show. Faculty had grown from 40 to nearly 70. The departments that had existed previously were strengthened, and new departments, such as chemical engineering, mechanical engineering, and civil engineering, were built from the ground up. In 1978, there were 363 undergraduates and 138 graduate students in engineering; by 1984, those numbers had risen to 568 and 228, respectively. Enrollment in part-time engineering programs doubled, and included 2,000 master's candidates. While only electrical engineering had been accredited at the School's outset, by 1985 accreditation had been won for six programs: electrical engineering, chemical engineering, materials science and engineering, biomedical engineering, engineering mechanics, and civil engineering. Externally funded research support for engineering faculty rose from $900,000 to more than $3 million in five years.

* * *

Additional faculty and students made even more imperative the need to upgrade the School's physical facilities, and a major program of renovation was undertaken. Slowly at first, but with gathering momentum, financial support from the corporate and industrial sector helped move an ambitious program off the drawing boards.

In 1981, the Department of Electrical Engineering and Computer Science (the new name was adopted to reflect more accurately the growing importance of the department's computer activities) opened a Microprocessor Laboratory and a Computer Graphics Facility with financial assistance from several corporations. The laboratory afforded state-of-the-art resources for instruction and research in this increasingly important field of engineering.

Also in 1981, the School established a new Engineering Computing Facility with highly advanced computers to serve the needs of all its departments. In 1984, the School received $2 million worth of computer equipment from AT&T Information Systems to support teaching and research, particularly in computer networking. In another arrangement with private industry, the School was given a large discount by Digital Equipment Corporation on 100 "top-of-the-line" microcomputers, which the School shared with other divisions of the University. IBM awarded $250,000 for further development of the computer science program.

Space in which to conduct the new programs and house the new equipment was also an urgent problem as the young School struggled through its critical formative years. Barton Hall, which had housed Electrical Engineering since its opening in 1962, was in good condition, but Maryland and Latrobe halls, which housed the other engineering activities, were among the oldest buildings on the Homewood campus and had never been substantially renovated.

Maryland Hall was tackled first. New laboratories were constructed for the Department of Materials Science and Engineering, the Department of Chemical Engineering, and the undergraduate program in biomedical engineering, and an addition was made to the building's second story. The first of three television classrooms was opened, affording students two-way audio and video communication with engineering courses given at the Applied Physics Laboratory.

Renovation of Latrobe Hall included two one-story wings to provide teaching and research laboratories for Mechanical Engineering and Civil Engineering, as well as new faculty and student offices, and a new plaza atop underground laboratory space. Care was taken to preserve the building's finely-crafted marble base, vaulted arches, and oak millwork.

Both renovations were assisted by major grants from the Pew Memorial Trust and the Kresge Foundation and by a $1.5 million gift from the State of Maryland, which has provided major support for engineering at Johns Hopkins from the school's earliest days.

Altogether in its first five years, the School of Engineering invested more than $10 million in new equipment and facilities renovation.

* * *

With the mainstream departments and administrative structure in place, the School was able to concentrate on developing particular areas of research which would give it uniqueness and character. In this effort, the School was able to build on traditional Hopkins strength in such areas as quantum electronics, environmental sciences (especially in water resources), materials science, mathematical theory and model-

Abel Wolman, world-renowned consultant on water resources and sanitation, was a member of the undergraduate Class of 1913. Seventy years later, he was still consulting on global water problems for the World Health Organization.

ing, and biomedical engineering. Newly recruited faculty brought to the School experts in chemical reactor design, structural safety, probability theory, aerodynamics, and thermal sciences.

Among the specialized facilities that were created and which attracted widespread attention was the Hopkins Center for Nondestructive Evaluation, established in 1984, which immediately drew interest and support from both government and industry. The center—an extension of the School's exceptionally strong program in the Department of Materials Science and Engineering—employed laser technology, ultrasonics, nuclear imaging, and other advanced techniques to search out defects in items as different as airplane wings and microchips—without pulling them apart. This work, again, involved a broad spectrum of scientific and engineering talent that crossed departmental and divisional University boundaries.

Similarly, Biomedical Engineering, which had been a department at the School of Medicine and Hospital since 1970, was obviously a field with strong crossover between medical and engineering technology. The department assumed responsibility for the popular undergraduate program in the Whiting School in 1980. Engineering research in this field included contributions to biomedical image analysis, neurosensory research instrumentation, clinical sensors and transducers, and computer-based clinical information systems.

* * *

One aspect of the exchanges that developed between the Whiting School and the corporate-industrial sector had nothing to do with contract research or gifts of money and hardware. In 1983, part-time engineering programs which had been under the Evening College were transferred to the School of Engineering. The graduate component was the largest program of its kind in the country, and it brought total Hopkins engineering enrollment—full-time and part-time—to more than 3,000 students.

Part-time programs continued to grow, both at Homewood and at the Applied Physics Laboratory's new Kossiakoff Center in Howard County. Growth was stimulated when television classrooms were opened at both locations. By 1984, the most popular part-time offering was a master's program in computer science, which attracted 850 students. In the fall of 1985, the School began offering graduate-level courses in computer science at the Army's Aberdeen Proving Ground in Harford County, 22 miles northeast of Baltimore. The program was open to all qualified military personnel as well as civilian employees and residents of nearby communities.

These part-time graduate programs provided a major service to the Baltimore area, which had no other school of engineering, and to the high-tech-saturated Washington suburbs through offerings at the Kossiakoff Center. They were especially important in a time when high starting salaries offered by industry were drawing off large numbers of engineering graduates who had only bachelor's degrees. Industry, in effect but of necessity, was eating its own seed corn. These young engineers needed the kind of further specialized training that part-time programs made possible.

* * *

On its fifth anniversary, the Whiting School took time out in November 1984 to reflect upon and celebrate the achievements of the first difficult years of engineering's "rebirth" at Johns Hopkins. There was a gala dinner for 500 faculty, alumni, and guests at Baltimore's Hyatt Regency Hotel that featured speeches and the presentation of the first G.W.C. Whiting School Medals to four people who were instrumental in the School's founding. Next day, there was a panel discussion of engineering's past, present, and future at the University, moderated by the venerable Abel Wolman, a 1913 alumnus, professor emeritus, and, at age 92, still actively consulting on water projects around the globe for the World Health Organization.

Characteristically, Dr. Wolman stamped his own unique perspective on the predictable optimism that the occasion generated. To add what he called a "flavor of dissent," he voiced concern about the writing and speaking skills of many young engineers, including those at Johns Hopkins, and urged that greater effort be made to link engineering with the humanities. In a later interview published in the School's annual report, Dr. Wolman said:

"We're traversing a world in which nothing any longer stands by itself. Nothing I touch can now do without the advances in materials. Nothing I touch can stand without oceanography, or hydrodynamics, or electronics. My message is this simple: Watch. Look at prospect, as well as retrospect. I hope the School will always find linkages, because that's where you find advance."

Seldom has the business of what Johns Hopkins was all about in the early years of its second century been more eloquently and succinctly expressed.

Research centers

In addition to research conducted through the various academic departments at Homewood, several autonomous research centers made valuable contributions to the work and reputation of Johns Hopkins over the years. In addition to the Humanities Center and the Center for Metropolitan Planning and Research already described, they included:

• Chesapeake Bay Institute. Founded shortly after World War II as the oceanographic and marine research division of Johns Hopkins, CBI, with the great Chesapeake serving as a living laboratory at its doorstep, became one of the world's most renowned centers for research in estuarine and coastal marine science. On its 30th anniversary in 1978, the Institute, for many years headed by noted oceanographer Donald W. Pritchard, was the largest of the Homewood-based research centers with 70 employees and an annual budget exceeding $2 million. The next year, the Institute moved to a seven-acre tract at Shady Side, Maryland, 15 miles south of Annapolis on the bay's western shore. The new site, a gift to the University from Gould Inc., was ideally suited for the Institute to continue its work, which ranged from theoretical research on fundamental estuarine processes to intensely practical studies of environmental pollution. CBI engaged in a number of programs in cooperation with other Johns Hopkins divisions, such as the Department of Environmental Health Sciences at the School of Hygiene and Public Health.

• Center for Social Organization of Schools. Funded primarily by the National Institute of Education, CSOS was established in the late 1960s with the general goal of making elementary and secondary schooling more effective. Located in a large residential building across Charles Street from the Homewood campus, the Center's team of sociologists and psychologists pioneered basic research on how the ways in which schools and classrooms were organized affected learning among students and the outcome of education later in life.

• Center for the Advancement of Academically Talented Youth. Building on a Johns Hopkins tradition of special concern for intellectually gifted young people that began with

The Ridgely Warfield *is a unique 106-foot catamaran that is part of a fleet of research vessels operated by the University's Chesapeake Bay Institute. Scientists and students at the Institute pursue basic research in all phases of estuarine science, using the Chesapeake and coastal waters of the Atlantic Ocean as a "living" laboratory.*

President Goodnow, the Center was founded in 1979 to identify and encourage boys and girls under age 13 with superior
academic ability. Through the Center and an earlier program,
the Study of Mathematically Precocious Youth founded in
1971 by Julian Stanley, professor of psychology, more than
10,000 youngsters across the country were tested, encouraged, and counseled through special programs at the University and via correspondence.

'Life-long learning'

A great deal can be inferred about the evolution of part-time education at Johns Hopkins from the names by which this endeavor has been known over the years. Starting in 1909 with College Courses for Teachers, the name progressed through the College for Teachers, McCoy College, and the Evening College and Summer Session. In 1984, the name was changed again to the School of Continuing Studies.

The newest change was proposed by Dean Stanley C. Gabor, former associate dean of the School of Continuing Education at New York University, who came to Hopkins in 1982 upon the retirement of Dean Roman J. Verhaalen after 12 years of outstanding service. The reasons for the change become apparent upon consideration of the development of the School in the decade following the University's centennial.

Although its essential mission—making valuable educational resources available to part-time students in the Baltimore-Washington area—remained the same, the School underwent dramatic shifts in its orientation during those years. It moved from an educational facility that was primarily undergraduate and pre-professional to one that was predominantly graduate and post-professional in nature. This transition is doubtless the most global change in the School's recent history, and it took place within the decade of the 1970s. The turnover year was 1975, when graduate en-

'Rapid change in society, especially that provoked by technology, has made it apparent that without renewal, vocational obsolescence would become nearly universal in almost all professions.'

rollment exceeded undergraduate for the first time. By 1980, enrollment was about 70 percent graduate and 30 percent undergraduate, exactly the reverse of what it had been ten years earlier.

Among the reasons for this transition was the School's

continuing development of graduate degree programs that were not available at Hopkins or elsewhere locally. These included the School's first doctoral program, an Ed.D. in human communications implemented in 1975 that was a milestone in continuing education. The doctorate was subsequently offered in counseling, technical management, and clinical education. Certificates of advanced study beyond the master's degree were also available in a number of areas.

A second major factor in the School's maturation was the inauguration of full-time faculty. At Hopkins and other institutions offering part-time education, part-time faculty had always been heavily—if not exclusively—relied on to carry out the teaching function. Echoing a 1969 recommendation by Dean Richard A. Mumma, a report the following year by a special committee appointed to examine future directions for the School recommended the recruiting of a small core of full-time faculty. The School's Academic Council moved quickly on the matter, and the first appointment was made in 1973. By 1983, there were 16 full-time faculty in teaching positions.

Results of the growing professionalization were soon evident. The Division of Education, the oldest of three degree-granting divisions in the School, became a leader in developing advanced programs. Largely through the work of Gilbert B. Schiffman, professor of education and coordinator of programs for exceptional children, the division gained wide recognition in the field of human communication and its disorders. Dr. Schiffman, who had taken leave to serve as head of the National Right to Read Program, returned in 1978 to implement an interdisciplinary program drawing upon the resources of both the School and the Kennedy Institute in East Baltimore. Through this and similar initiatives, the division became nationally known for its training programs in teaching the handicapped and for the application of new technology, such as computers, in this area.

The Division of Administration and Business, which for many years had offered standard programs in finance and economics, in the late 1970s began extending its courses into accounting, administrative science, advertising, business law, management, marketing, real estate, and urban planning and policy management, the last in cooperation with the Center for Metropolitan Planning and Research. New directions included a unique graduate program known as the Hopkins Fellows Program in Community and Organizational Change. Designed for corporate executives, government officials, community leaders, and others wishing to develop skills in change management, the program applied techniques of behavioral science to organization and community change efforts.

The Division of Arts and Sciences continued to present a broad range of programs in the arts, humanities, and physical and social sciences, including its unique response to the changing cultural and intellectual needs of adults—the Master of Liberal Arts program. The division also maintained its long-standing commitment to undergraduate programs for students in liberal arts and pre-engineering fields.

Continuing Education, a fourth division of the School which serves non-degree students whose interests lie in career advancement or personal enrichment, called increasingly on the resources of the degree-granting divisions and other Hopkins units to provide an extensive menu of both traditional and interdisciplinary subjects of current concern.

* * *

Enrollment in the School remained fairly steady during the 1970s and early 1980s, despite the on-going transition from an undergraduate to a graduate population. Total 1970-1980 registrations fluctuated from a low of 6,218 in 1972 to a high of 7,268 in 1980. The latter figure was below the all-time high of more than 7,400 reached in the mid-1960s. National economic ups and downs and growing competition for part-time students from state-supported community colleges and other regional schools were factors in the enrollment pattern of the period. Still, the School of Continuing Studies remained the largest of all the Johns Hopkins divisions in numbers of students, and the only division that was financially self-supporting.

Enrollment in the School's summer sessions averaged 2,700 a year for the decade. Teachers and other education professionals continued to make up a large percentage of the summer student body but, increasingly, the summer sessions came to serve adult students enrolled in the fall and spring sessions and became, in effect, the School's trimester.

* * *

One of the new directions in which there was major movement during this period was a broadening of the School's geographic base in order to make its programs more accessible to students outside the immediate Baltimore area. The center at the Applied Physics Laboratory, the oldest of a number of off-campus ventures, remained the most successful, enrolling in 1982 more than 1,400 students.

The center in Columbia, Maryland, which stressed programs in business, education, and applied behavioral sciences, was also highly successful. In 1984, ten years after its opening, the Columbia center moved into a new building with expanded classroom space and greatly improved facilities, including a computing center and provision for a television classroom where courses taught at Homewood could be received. The number of students enrolled during the center's first ten years rose from 32 to more than 800.

Along with its growing professionalism and with rising recognition of its leadership in special education and other fields, the School began to win substantially increased outside financial support. The National Endowment for the Humanities, the U.S. Department of Education, the Bureau of Education for the Handicapped, the Hodson Trust, and the Maryland Vocational Rehabilitation Division were among contributors of major grants or contracts. Alumni support also increased, reaching more than $95,000 in 1983. The School appointed its first full-time director of development and alumni relations in 1984; earlier, advertising and publications had become the responsibility of a newly created Office of Public Affairs.

* * *

Just as broader access was one hallmark of part-time education at Johns Hopkins, flexibility was another, as seen in the rapid response by the School to changing needs in professional fields as diverse as mental retardation and computer science. Flexibility became even more important during the 1970s as a major new focus developed, one which affected not only the School of Continuing Studies but the entire University. President Muller had spoken of the idea of "life-long learning" in his centennial dinner address in 1976, and it was a main point in a report six years later by another review committee examining future directions for the School.

The report cited clear evidence that part-time education for adults would become increasingly important in American colleges and universities. "Bunching 'all' the educational experiences of an individual into eight years is both peda-gogically dubious and economically impossible in some instances," the report said. "Rapid change in society, espe-cially that provoked by technology, has made it apparent that without renewal, vocational obsolescence would become nearly universal in almost all professions. Part-time educa-tion is essential if individuals are to keep abreast of new knowledge in their areas of expertise."

When he took office in 1982, Dean Gabor began to lead

The Johns Hopkins School of Continuing Studies has expanded its activities to several locations off the main Baltimore campus in an effort to meet growing needs among adults for professional advancement and personal enrichment. The School's new center in Columbia, Maryland, is located in this building.

the School even further beyond the scope usually associated with part-time education enterprises. He reemphasized the classic Hopkins posture of concentrating on areas of special strength and not attempting to be all things to all people, and in addition turned new attention to the requirements of an emerging postprofessional society. Graduate programs were expanded and new weekend and summer formats were developed. In the non-credit area, Saturday courses in foreign languages—such as modern Greek and Japanese—were begun, and offerings in communications were increased, including publishing workshops developed with the Johns Hopkins University Press. The number of non-credit courses was doubled, moving into art, music, film, creative writing, and natural history. And at Commencement in May 1985, the School held its first separate diploma ceremony for its own degree recipients, a long-standing practice of other academic divisions of Johns Hopkins.

It was to reflect the School's growing graduate orientation and its expanded schedule that Dean Gabor sought to change the name. The idea was approved, and its logic helped win general acceptance. In his March 1984 letter to alumni, parents, and friends, President Muller wrote: "Building on a 75-year tradition of part-time education in the Baltimore-Washington corridor, the School of Continuing Studies sees an unprecedented opportunity to provide adult students with the diverse academic programs they need for professional and personal enrichment. The new name more accurately describes the commitment of the School, and, indeed, the entire University, to life-long learning."

* * *

In July 1985, Dr. Muller announced a major new venture in part-time graduate education, an agreement with officials of Montgomery County, Maryland, for Johns Hopkins to establish a facility at the Shady Grove Life Sciences Center northwest of Washington. To be known as the Johns Hopkins Center for Advanced Studies in Montgomery County, Md., the center was intended to serve the graduate and professional educational needs of the county's large population of high-technology and science-oriented residents.

On a 38-acre campus given to Johns Hopkins by the county, the University planned to open in temporary quarters in the summer of 1986, offering master's degree programs in computer science, electrical engineering, and technical management through the part-time program of the G.W.C. Whiting School of Engineering. Also under consideration were courses and special training programs to be offered by the School of Continuing Studies, the School of Arts and Sciences, and the School of Hygiene and Public Health.

Creation of the new center was supported by a survey by the University and the Montgomery County Office of Economic Development, which showed an overwhelmingly positive response from scientists and engineers in corporations and government laboratories in the county. Among the latter are the National Bureau of Standards, the U.S. Department of Energy, and the National Institutes of Health.

Medicine's old order changeth

The Johns Hopkins Medical Institutions in the years following the University's centennial maintained and in many areas enhanced their preeminent status in each of their primary historic roles: education, research, and patient care.

It was a period highlighted by completion of a ten-year, $150 million rebuilding program, by the winning of a Nobel Prize by two Hopkins investigators, by realignment of priorities in the admission and education of medical students, by a restructuring of medical specialties, and by innovative responses to fundamental changes that were taking place in the basic system of health care delivery in the United States.

The building program has been described in detail; not discussed was how it benefited from the joint Hospital-University presidency assumed by Dr. Muller in 1972. Patient care, research, and teaching were traditionally inseparable at Hopkins, and more than one-third of all the Hospital's facilities were used for teaching and research by the medical faculty of the University.

As chief executive of both institutions, President Muller was in a position to oversee the entire project and ensure that all facets of the redevelopment were coordinated.

He was also able to monitor research areas in which two or more Hopkins divisions were involved. Cancer research is a good example, with both clinical and basic research being done at the medical institutions, basic cancer

153

In the education of young men and women for careers in modern medicine, Hopkins continued the example of innovation and creative experimentation that had marked its programs from their beginnings nearly a century before.

biology at Homewood, and other aspects of the disease of interest at the School of Hygiene and Public Health. In his report on Dr. Muller's first ten years in office, trustees' chairman Robert D.H. Harvey described the joint presidency as "one of the most beneficial aspects of the decade."

* * *

"I'm very happy to hear it, but I'll need to get some confirmation," said Daniel Nathans. Hamilton O. Smith's response was simply, "Holy cow!" That is how two professors in the Department of Microbiology who had spent their entire careers at Johns Hopkins reacted to early-morning phone calls on October 12, 1978, advising them that they had just won the Nobel Prize for Medicine. The champagne corks were already popping when the two arrived at their labs a short time later. There was hardly a soul throughout the University who did not share the pride and excitement that swept the East Baltimore campus that day.

Daniel Nathans, left, receives the 1978 Nobel Prize for Medicine, which he shared with another Johns Hopkins scientist, Hamilton O. Smith, and Swiss researcher Werner Arber. They were honored for research on restriction enzymes which made possible the new science of genetic engineering.

The work for which Drs. Nathans and Smith were honored (they shared the prize with Swiss researcher Werner Arber) had to do with restriction enzymes, which have been described as "biological scissors" that can slice into a chain of DNA—the biological molecules that carry the genetic codes for all living things—at specific points, making it possible to understand the complex geometry of the DNA sequence and also to create segments that can be recombined in different ways. Arber had postulated the existence of such enzymes; Smith discovered the first one outside the theoretical realm; Nathans demonstrated that cleavage at specific points takes place.

The implications of this work for the science of genetics were staggering—some even compared it with the first splitting of the atom. The discovery of restriction enzymes opened the entirely new field of genetic engineering, popularly called gene-splicing. This, in turn, enabled scientists to make a quantum leap in techniques for mapping the sequence of genes in normal cells and provided entirely new tools for approaching at the molecular level such diseases as cancer, sickle cell anemia, and other genetic abnormalities. The discovery also made possible within a few years the mass production of interferon, insulin, and growth hormones; better crop yields; and improved industrial plastics.

A second far-reaching advance made by Hopkins medical research during this period was a technique to identify neurotransmitters, the brain's chemical messengers, and their receptors or binding sites—showing how, in effect, nerve cells in the brain "talked" to each other. The work, a contribution of psychopharmacologist Solomon H. Snyder, was hailed as fundamental in solving problems in such areas as pain relief and narcotics addiction. For it, Dr. Snyder received the 1978 Albert Lasker Basic Medical Research Award. In 1980, he was named to head a new Department of Neuroscience.

Dr. Snyder's studies went back 12 years to when he and a young graduate student, Candace Pert, first demonstrated sites in nervous tissue where opiates acted. They then showed that the brain itself produced morphine-like substances known as enkephalins that attached to the opiate receptors; the press coined the term, "the brain's own morphine" and, indeed, the discovery offered hope of explaining the mechanism of addiction to morphine and other opium derivatives.

Dr. Snyder and a team of researchers continued to build upon this concept of specific receptors geared to specific molecules and the chemical nature of neurotransmission. In 1975, Dr. Snyder was able to report that antischizophrenic drugs worked by blocking the brain's receptors for a neurotransmitter called dopamine, and a new blood test was devised that permitted physicians to avoid administering either useless underdoses or dangerous overdoses of the drugs. Another dramatic "first" was the use of positron emission tomography by a Hopkins team to map opiate receptors in a living human brain. An article in the Winter 1984 issue of *Hopkins Medical News* provided this perspective: "The work is of importance not only as a demonstration that receptors in humans can be visualized but because the chemical techniques can be applied to many other receptors. These structures on the cell surface play an important role in a host of diseases and are the sites where all drugs elicit both therapeutic and side effects." The door was thus opened for direct monitoring of drug therapy—a second-by-second picture of where and how drugs acted in the brain—and for a new assault on such degenerative neurological diseases as myasthenia gravis, Parkinson's disease, Down's syndrome, and Alzheimer's disease.

* * *

Another traditional area of research strength at Hopkins which saw major gains during this period was cardiology. The opening of the new Clayton Heart Center climaxed a decade of advance in the diagnosis and treatment of heart ailments in which Hopkins researchers played a part. One example was the final report of the Coronary Primary Prevention Trial, a multi-institution study which answered decades-old questions about the role of dietary cholesterol and established that lowering cholesterol levels in the bloodstream decreased the risk of heart attacks. In another example, t-PA (tissue plasminogen activator) came into use as a safer method than existing therapies for dissolving clots in coronary arteries in acute thrombosis; the drug was produced by genetic engineering techniques made possible by the action of restriction enzymes. A technique called balloon valvuloplasty developed by Hopkins physicians replaced open-heart surgery in as many as 1,000 children a year. An implantable automatic defibrillator was developed, as were other major weapons against sudden death among heart patients.

In cardiac surgery—a field which had been founded at Hopkins by Alfred Blalock and Helen Taussig with the famous "blue baby" procedure—operations were being performed at the rate of 800 a year in 1983. Heart surgery that year came under the direction of Bruce Reitz, who had performed the first successful heart-lung transplantation. Dr. Reitz inaugurated a new Heart and Heart-Lung Transplant Service at Hopkins which marked the crumbling of an old barrier—transplant rejection. A new drug, cyclosporine (in the testing of which Dr. Reitz had played a major role), showed unusual promise in preventing rejection without destroying a patient's ability to fight bacterial infection, an often-fatal consequence of earlier drugs. In 1985, surgeons performed Hopkins' first dual heart-kidney transplant on a 20-year-old Randallstown, Maryland, woman that transformed her in less than a month from an invalid with only weeks to live to a happy person who could "ride" 15 miles a day on a stationary bicycle.

* * *

The research advances in psychopharmacology and cardiology described above are not only significant in their own right, but they also exemplify the thread of continuity and demonstrate the value of long, patient scholarship that are hallmarks of Hopkins medicine. Other highlights of the 1977-1985 period include the following:

1977—The University risked the loss of up to $700,000 a year in federal funds by rejecting a condition of eligibility that would have required it to admit a government-set quota of Americans who had begun their medical education abroad. Hopkins was joined by several other leading medical schools in its defense of its right to select its own students, and

Congress amended the program to the extent that its provisions were no longer objectionable.

1980—At the dedication of the Cancer Center's new radiation therapy wing, it was announced that radiation oncology director Stanley Order had developed a new radio-immuno-therapy technique using polyclonal antibodies to deliver doses of radiation to tumors via the bloodstream, a system that showed dramatic results in treating victims of liver cancer.

1981—Studies in the Oncology Center showed that a new drug, acyclovir, was effective in preventing the growth of several viruses in humans, including the herpes simplex virus. The nation's first Swallowing Center was established at Johns Hopkins to deal in an interdisciplinary fashion with the variety of disorders that cause swallowing problems.

158

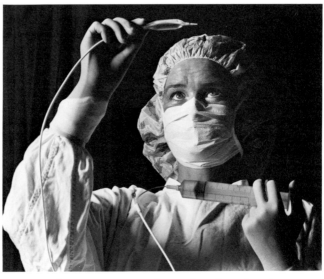

Balloon catheterization is one of a number of non-invasive diagnostic or treatment techniques developed by Johns Hopkins medical researchers. This procedure eliminated the need for open-heart surgery in thousands of children suffering from pulmonary valve stenosis, a narrowing of the valve which controls heart-lung blood flow.

1982—The first artificial knee which allowed the patient's bone cells to grow into the prosthesis was successfully tested in patients. By creating a mathematical model of the immune system, investigators determined that a simple mechanism—the immunon theory—could explain how cells began to produce antibodies. Ophthalmologists developed a new laser treatment that was highly effective in preventing senile macular degeneration, a leading cause of blindness.

1983—Urologist Patrick C. Walsh announced a new technique for removing cancerous prostate glands that did not leave patients impotent, as the first radical prostatectomy, developed in 1904 by another Hopkins urologist, Hugh H. Young, often did.

1984—Hopkins scientists announced a new way to relieve the nausea frequently associated with cancer chemotherapy; a promising treatment for certain genetic storage disorders, utilizing bone marrow transplantation; a new diet treatment for kidney failure; vitamin therapy for a congenital form of dementia; and a new technique for making highly sensitive monoclonal antibodies, substances with a vast potential for diagnosing and treating a wide range of diseases.

1985—The National Institute on Aging selected Hopkins as the site and awarded a $5 million grant for one of five Alzheimer's Disease Research Centers, recognition of the existing leadership and commitment of Hopkins in the area of problems of aging. At the other end of the life spectrum, the first Maryland baby conceived through a new Hopkins in vitro fertilization program—a six-pound boy—was born in February.

* * *

In the education of young men and women for careers in modern medicine, Hopkins continued the example of innovation and creative experimentation that had marked its programs from their beginnings nearly a century before. In the early 1980s, the School of Medicine was accepting an average of 125 first-year students each September from an applicant pool of as many as 3,000. They were facing a long commitment to incredibly intensive work, the first four years of which would cost them close to $65,000. More than 60 percent would require financial aid, but would still graduate with average debts of $40,000. The ability to provide scholarship support to assure that the best-qualified students could come to Hopkins—regardless of their income—was a continuing concern at the School and the subject of increasing fund-raising efforts as federal support in this area reached a plateau and even appeared vulnerable to reduction.

Of equal concern was a national trend that emerged in the late 1970s, when the number of young physicians considering research or teaching as careers began to decline. To an institution that had been the first in the country to integrate the applications of research and lecture room training with patient care and that had built a worldwide reputation for doing so, this development reinforced a determination to expose its students to both the rigors and joys of research and to enable those who so wished to pursue that course. This was a matter of special interest to Richard S. Ross, a distinguished cardiologist and professor of medicine who, in the fall of 1975, had succeeded Dr. Morgan as dean of the School of Medicine and vice president for the University's health divisions. Dr. Ross was pleased a few years later to be able to report that the Hopkins tradition was holding firm: whereas a national survey indicated that only 3.5 percent of graduating medical students said they wanted to teach and only a "handful" planned to do research, a similar survey at Hopkins showed that 51 percent of the seniors intended to devote themselves to clinical teaching and investigation and another 4.5 percent to basic science teaching and research.

* * *

Another concern shared by Dr. Ross and others on the Hopkins faculty and by President Muller had to do with what was known as "premed syndrome," the tendency among undergraduates planning to enter medical school to pack their curricula with science courses, the better to impress admissions officers. Once in medical school, these young people were enmeshed in even more narrowly focused courses and, as a result, often failed to develop as well-rounded individuals.

Dr. Muller enjoyed a unique perspective on this and other

problems relating to medical education. For three years beginning in 1981, he headed an 18-member panel which conducted an intensive examination of medical students' education and their college preparation for the Association of American Medical Colleges. In September 1984, the group issued its report titled "Physicians for the Twenty-First Century," which contained 27 recommendations for change. Chief among them were that broad study in the natural and social sciences and in the humanities be required of all students; that medical schools should regard applicants who have pursued a wide range of studies equally with those who have concentrated on science; and that medical schools should impart to students the skills they will need throughout their careers for continuing independent learning.

Many of the panel's recommendations were already in place or under development at Hopkins. A major effort to counter the premed syndrome trend, for example, was instituted in 1983. Known as FlexMed, it was designed as a bridge between undergraduate work and medical school, encouraging students to defer matriculation in medical school for as long as two years in order to take courses in whatever interested them, study abroad, or even work if they wished. "We have set as our target the replication of physicians who will perpetuate the principles of the 'art of medicine' for which this great institution is known," wrote Dean Ross in his letter to colleagues and friends that summer.

Two years later, in the spring of 1985, the School carried this effort a giant step further. Hopkins became the first major medical school in the country to drop the requirement that applicants take the science-weighted MCAT, the standardized Medical College Admissions Test that had been in general use throughout the country since 1930. Surveys had shown that the MCAT had a more compromising effect on the undergraduate education of future physicians than any other component of the medical school admissions process. By eliminating it as a requirement, Hopkins hoped to dampen the fierce competition for high science grades among premedical students and to encourage them not to sacrifice the opportunity to get a good general education just to enhance their chances of gaining acceptance into medical school.

This effort to bring a new humane and social dimension to medical education was not confined to those just entering the field. As early as 1977, President Muller decided that a strong program should be mounted to make the arts and humanities more accessible to the entire medical community, in the "heart-and-head" tradition of Welch and Osler. Thus was formed the Committee on Cultural and Social Affairs, a cross-campus initiative headed by professor emeritus of neurosurgery George B. Udvarhelyi and Humanities Center director Richard Macksey. It began bringing a procession of prominent artists, musicians, and performers before enthusiastic and ever-growing East Baltimore audiences—notables such as violinist Isaac Stern, editor Norman Cousins, anthropologist Richard Leakey, Nobelists Francis Crick and Isaac Bashevis Singer, and actors John Houseman and Geraldine

162

Patient Tilman Walther (front, center) and some of the more than 100 staff members who made up the Johns Hopkins Heart/Lung Transplantation Service in the mid-1980s. Inaugurated in 1983 under the direction of Bruce Reitz, the service focuses the skills of not only cardiologists and cardiac surgeons but nurses, operating room technicians, physical therapists, social workers, and other specialists in evaluating potential transplant recipients and assisting them and their families through all stages of the complex procedure.

Fitzgerald. The program of symposia, seminars, and performances in 1984 was awarded a $200,000 grant from the National Endowment for the Humanities and became a model for similar efforts at other major medical centers.

Another aspect of changing conditions in medical education was addressed by a task force headed by Dr. Heyssel for the Commonwealth Fund. In its report issued in November 1985, the group described an ongoing "revolution" in the economics of medical care in the United States in which cost-consciousness and demands of the marketplace were placing unprecedented pressures on the nation's teaching hospitals. Calling for an overhaul of medical education and academic hospitals, the group cited such problems as over-production of specialists and a shortage of physicians in such areas as internal medicine, family practice, and pediatrics— areas of treatment where future demands will be greatest. The report also described a threat to teaching hospitals by the high cost of educating residents and the rapid growth of lower-cost alternative forms of medical care.

* * *

As it had always been, Hopkins medicine in the 1970s and 1980s was a dynamic, ever-changing enterprise that both led and responded to trends in medical education and research worldwide. Some of the new problems were direct results of previous success in preventing, improving the treatment of, or curing diseases that had been fatal in the past—problems associated with an aging population and with chronic ailments such as cancer, arthritis, and debilitating neurological disorders. Other new concerns were related to changing economic conditions and new priorities among both public and private supporters of medical science.

Slowly but continuously, the academic framework that had given the institution its strength and direction changed. Some of these changes led to the establishment of new departments such as Molecular Biology, Neuroscience, and Dermatology. Other departments acquired new names, including Anesthesiology and Critical Care Medicine, and Cell Biology and Anatomy. New specialties grew in importance within the existing framework: Comparative Medicine, Emergency Medicine, Genetics, Immunology, Laboratory Medicine, Perinatology, Rehabilitation Medicine, and Transplantation Surgery.

* * *

The developing field of the neurosciences perhaps best exemplified the direction of the evolutionary flow of Hopkins medicine during this period. It was also a persuasive demonstration of the value of the reintegration of knowledge concept—the bringing together of a number of specialties to focus on a particular problem area. This was a field to which the University could apply the talents of premier investigators like Vernon Mountcastle, a Lasker and Helmholtz award winner who had set the foundations for modern understanding of the workings of the cerebral cortex; world renowned neurologist Guy McKhann; Richard T. Johnson, an expert on viruses that affect the nervous system; director of psychiatry Paul R. McHugh; neurosurgeon-in-chief Donlin Long; Dr. Snyder and his team, and others. Skills running the spectrum from basic pharmacology to neurosurgery were ably represented, and an unusual opportunity existed for Hopkins medicine to combine them for maximum effectiveness.

The opening of the Adolf Meyer Center for Psychiatry and the Neurosciences in October 1982 made available the latest facilities for research and patient care in psychiatry, neurology, and neurosurgery—the three basic specialties dealing with the human brain. It contained a new Center for Neurological Diseases, the Henry Phipps Psychiatric Services, and an operating room with the latest automated equipment. In 1985, on the building's seventh floor, a new $500,000 Neurosciences Critical Care Unit was opened—the first of its kind in the country to offer patients with life-threatening brain and spinal cord diseases or injuries a unique combination of specialists and the most advanced monitoring and life-support equipment available in a single unit. Among other specialized facilities was the latest in nuclear imaging equipment, which enhanced Hopkins' reputation as a leading center for neuroradiology and nuclear medicine.

The new emphasis in Hopkins medicine represented by the Meyer Center was seen in other specialties as well—

oncology, cardiology, geriatrics, and trauma. The focus was on major diseases, rather than traditional medical disciplines. This was reflected not only in the departmental realignments but in the design of new facilities, which clustered the resources of all relevant medical disciplines around a problem. In the Hospital, physicians were thus able to address human ills with a conglomerate of specialists, breaking away from the compartmentalization philosophy which had served well in the past but was not geared to take full advantage of modern techniques and technology.

In an interview in the October 1980 issue of the *Johns Hopkins Magazine,* President Muller touched on the naturalness of this major development taking place at Hopkins: "I am struck by the fact that we are physically building an academic revolution of a kind in East Baltimore, by focusing our construction on diseases rather than on traditional disciplines. ... If I had come into office in 1972 and said we're going to take the Department of Psychiatry out of Phipps and put it in a new tower with neurology and neurosurgery, people would have thought I was crazy. And we didn't deliberately set out to do it; the medical faculty did the thinking and planning which made it seem inevitable."

* * *

As valuable as the joint University-Hospital presidency had been, Dr. Muller in 1983 stepped down from the post of Hospital chief executive. Dr. Heyssel, who had served as executive vice president and director of the Hospital since 1972, was named president of The Johns Hopkins Hospital. At the same time, the trustees of the University and Hospital created a joint Trustee Policy Committee to formulate and recommend policy and planning initiatives for both institutions. Dr. Muller was chairman of the committee, to which each board appointed five members, and was still intimately involved in policy making and coordination, but he felt that the two institutions had been working well together and that he need not continue to carry the title of Hospital president.

The most important aspect of improved University-Hospital coordination was the tremendous increase in explicitly joint activity between the two institutions, Dr. Muller said in an interview in 1985. As an example, he cited a program begun in 1983 to make the neighborhood around the East Baltimore campus as stable and attractive as possible by improving housing in a 15-block area. The project was a partnership among Hopkins, Baltimore City, the State of Maryland, private developers, lending institutions, and community groups. Residents were assisted in renovating existing properties and new homes were built on vacant lots. "We hope to see a racially mixed and Hopkins/non-Hopkins mixed neighborhood develop," Dr. Muller said, "one that has some of the flavor of what was around Hopkins before World War II, when people who worked there actually lived there."

Other examples of joint University-Hospital ventures reflected the institutions' response to rapid and sweeping changes in the economics of health care delivery. In 1984, Baltimore City transferred ownership of its financially troubled Baltimore City Hospitals to Johns Hopkins. Hopkins had

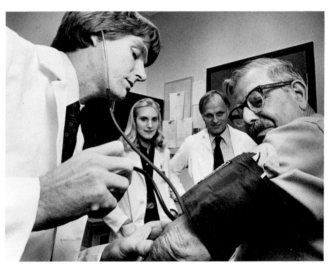

A tradition of attention to debilitating neurological and other disorders that often accompany old age led, in 1985, to the awarding to Johns Hopkins of a $5 million grant from the National Institute on Aging and to the selection of the University as one of five national Alzheimer's Disease Research Centers.

a long relationship with City Hospitals, training medical students and conducting research there and, starting in 1982, managing it through a subsidiary, Broadway Management Corporation. The name of the newly acquired facility was changed to the Francis Scott Key Medical Center, but it continued to function as a community hospital and regional burn center. Both Hopkins and the city contributed money for improvements, and Hopkins was given authority to develop 134 acres around the center as a biomedical park.

In 1985, the Medical Institutions took a major step in line with changing patterns of health care delivery by establishing a new health maintenance organization known as the Johns Hopkins Health Plan. While earlier Hopkins plans had served residents of East Baltimore and Columbia, the new plan offered residents throughout the metropolitan area access to the Hopkins system of health care and comprehensive services for a fixed, cost-competitive fee. Members enrolled through employer benefit contracts and were able to choose personal physicians, initially at any of 11 centers or physician group practices. "This HMO expands our historic mission to deliver the best medical care at a time of serious and well-placed public concern over the quality and cost of health care," commented Dr. Heyssel in the *Johns Hopkins Gazette* of August 6.

The plan extended Hopkins services beyond East Baltimore without any new construction, using instead a network of affiliated physicians and existing facilities in the metropolitan area. Among them was the Wyman Park Health System, a health maintenance-type facility located in the former U.S. Public Health Service Hospital adjacent to the Homewood campus. The Hospital and University began negotiating an agreement to bring Wyman Park into the family of Johns Hopkins Medical Institutions which would permit it to retain its own identity, at the same time building upon its strengths in meeting community needs and serving as a major site for the new Hopkins health plan.

Also in 1985, an affiliation was announced between Johns Hopkins Hospital and North Charles General Hospital, a small facility three blocks south of the Homewood campus. While continuing to function as a separate acute-care hospital, North Charles General was intended to serve additionally as a midtown clinic for the new Hopkins HMO. Also, noted Dr. Heyssel, Hopkins medical students and residents would be able to take part of their training at North Charles General, which carried a more representative caseload than the Hopkins Hospital with its large number of admissions for cardiac surgery, cancer treatment, and other advanced procedures.

The rebirth of nursing

The education of nurses, a logical adjunct to the education of physicians, started at Johns Hopkins with a class of 17 students in 1889, the same year that the Hospital opened and the same year the School of Medicine had been scheduled to open. The medical school was delayed by financial constraints, however, and did not open its doors until 1893, two years after the School of Nursing graduated its first class.

Among those graduates was M. Adelaide Nutting, who became the nursing school's principal and who was known for her strong belief that nursing programs should give nurses an education, not just prepare them to render hospital services. She was among the first to declare that nurses should get a college degree, not simply a diploma. Before she left for Columbia University to become the country's first professor of nursing and found the first nursing graduate program, she proposed in 1915 that Hopkins nurses raise an endowment for an independent, degree-granting school of nursing.

The nurses took up the challenge, formidable as it was, with an every-little-bit-counts attitude; nurses who earned $100 a month, for example, contributed 50 cents of that to what came to be known as the Nutting Fund. By 1929, they had raised $112,000, impressive but well short of their original goal of $1 million. Meanwhile, the Hopkins School of Nursing continued as it had begun, awarding diplomas, not Bachelor of Science in Nursing degrees.

... the trustees made a decision that Hopkins nursing alumnae had long awaited. A new School of Nursing would be established, offering a curriculum with intensive clinical training leading to a bachelor of nursing degree.

As in medicine, changes in the nursing profession came steadily in the wake of scientific and technological advances. By the 1960s, nurses were finding that a baccalaureate degree was essential for professional advancement. Interest in diploma programs declined and, in 1973, after 84 years of operation, the Johns Hopkins School of Nursing closed.

The moment was not so dark as it might seem, for there was an innovative plan for the University's new School of Health Services to begin offering the long-sought baccalaureate in nursing, which it did in the fall of 1975. It was a two-year, upper-division program for students who had completed two years of college. Thirty-two students, including four men, enrolled in the first year. The Nutting Fund by this time had grown to nearly $800,000, enough to endow a chair in the new School. Candidates were being interviewed as the first group of students graduated in 1977; the class chose caps and pins similar to those worn by graduates of the former Hopkins Hospital program.

Nursing's victory in attaining degree status proved to be short-lived, as the School of Health Services fell upon hard financial times and was closed in the summer of 1978, except for those who were due to receive their degrees the following year. At the time, President Muller announced that the University was launching an immediate planning effort to honor its commitment to nursing education by establishing a financially viable program at the postbaccalaureate level. Meanwhile, the Nutting Fund portfolio continued to build, but it had neither a school nor a program to support.

To help bridge the gap, the Evening College in 1980 revitalized its baccalaureate degree program for registered nurses. The following year, Carol J. Gray, former associate dean of the School of Nursing at the University of Texas Health Science Center, was named director of the Division of Nursing at the Evening College. As an added responsibility, she was charged with preparing a proposal for a new, two-year upper division nursing program to be offered by Hopkins in conjunction with several other area hospitals.

In February 1983, the University trustees made a decision that Hopkins nursing alumnae had long awaited. A new School of Nursing would be established, offering a curriculum with intensive clinical training leading to a bachelor of nursing degree. The School was to open in the fall of 1984, with a graduate program to commence as soon as it was financially feasible. In order to make the new venture possible, the University and three Baltimore hospitals—Hopkins, Sinai, and Church—joined in a novel enterprise and formed the Consortium for Nursing Education Inc. to operate the School. Dr. Gray was named as dean.

In his letter to alumni, parents, and friends in February 1983, President Muller commented on the turn of events following the closing of the original School with its emphasis on clinical training: "Since that time there has been a move nationwide toward a more academic and theoretical approach to nursing education. We see merit in both approaches, and expect the new school to achieve a blend that will again provide a national model." He also noted that the

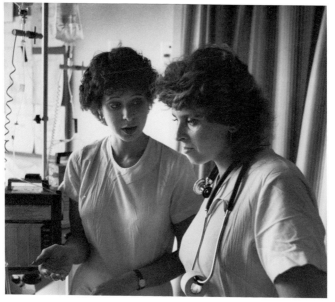

The Consortium for Nursing Education, Inc., a unique model for the modern training of nurses, established a new Johns Hopkins University School of Nursing in 1984, continuing a tradition that dates back to 1889. Operated in affiliation with three Baltimore hospitals, the School offers a two-year Bachelor of Science degree program.

three participating hospitals had agreed to take responsibility for the School's fiscal integrity, thus assuring both long-term funding and no new burden on limited general University revenues. That point was crucial, because the University could not have undertaken such a venture on its own.

* * *

On September 5, 1984, the new School of Nursing opened in renovated quarters in the Phipps Building of Johns Hopkins Hospital, and the Evening College began phasing out its degree program for registered nurses. At dedication ceremonies on September 23, the establishment of the M. Adelaide Nutting Chair, the School's first endowed professorship, was announced. The fund by that time had grown to $1.5 million, and now it had a place to go. The long effort to create this chair was an example of professional dedication of the highest order, and it was the first chair in the University's history to be endowed by an alumni group. Named to the new chair was Elaine Larson, the holder of a B.S.N., an M.A. in nursing, and a doctoral degree in epidemiology from the University of Washington in Seattle and a nationally known expert in critical care nursing.

In its first year, the new School provided an excellent example of collaboration among University divisions. While the broad range of nursing courses was taught by the School's faculty, courses in pharmacology, pathophysiology, computer technology, and nutrition were taught by faculty from the School of Medicine and the School of Hygiene and Public Health. In the spring of 1985, elective courses at the Homewood divisions were made available to School of Nursing students.

Other attractions included the opportunity for students to do clinical rotations and take part in special programs at all three participating hospitals. Church Hospital, for example, ran a hospice program; Sinai, a special program in rehabilitation medicine; Hopkins offered strength in oncology and pediatric medicine. The School also placed strong emphasis on new biomedical technology and had its own computer laboratory to help students utilize computer data in clinical decision-making.

Attention was given to traditional values in Hopkins nursing, such as a high regard for patient care and humane practice. Nurses were also trained for new roles thrust upon the profession by changing patterns of health care delivery, such as the need to prepare patients and their families for more elaborate home care, the result of a growing trend toward shorter in-patient stays.

Dr. Muller expressed his enthusiasm for the concept of the new School in the *Johns Hopkins Magazine* in October 1983: "An institution with such a leadership tradition in medicine should be well-qualified—almost obligated—to have a leadership tradition in nursing. . . . The fact that the three hospitals in the consortium have in effect agreed to underwrite it, I think is just marvelous. It gives the University an opportunity to do something that the hospitals cannot do for themselves —they cannot grant degrees. And at the same time it allows Hopkins to get back into nursing education with the full capability, if we do it right, of mounting a program at the level of national leadership."

* * *

In 1985, the renovated Phipps Building partially occupied by the School was renamed the Frank M. Houck Building in recognition of the generosity of a 1915 graduate of the School of Medicine who never practiced medicine but served as assistant director of The Johns Hopkins Hospital from 1927 to 1942. Dr. Houck, who died in 1976, left the Hospital 1,000 acres of land near Colorado Springs, Colorado, recently valued at several million dollars.

Public health's 'Second Revolution'

Between 1975 and 1985, age brought on the closely spaced retirements not only of the dean but of heads of all but one of the 11 departments at the School of Hygiene and Public Health. The fact that the School was able to survive this mass exodus of talent and experience without losing momentum and, in addition, to emerge in a configuration needed to deal with extremely rapid changes in the field, is a tribute to the man chosen as Dean Hume's successor, Donald A. Henderson, and to the team of public health experts he assembled to lead the institution.

A 1960 alumnus of the School and the holder of an M.D. degree from the University of Rochester, Dr. Henderson came to the dean's office in 1977 from the World Health Organization, where he was head of the worldwide Smallpox Eradication Program that succeeded in eliminating this ancient scourge, the first such achievement in medical history. (Among the honors recognizing his contribution were the Special Albert Lasker Public Health Service Award in 1976 and the 1985 Albert Schweitzer International Prize for Medicine.)

Dr. Henderson took over the School during an era that professionals in the field were calling the Second Public Health Revolution. Whereas the first revolution had seen such advances as the provision of safe drinking

The field of public health in the early 1980s demonstrated perhaps better than any other major Hopkins activity the swelling current of interdisciplinary studies at the University.

water through chlorination, the pasteurization of milk, and immunization against life-threatening diseases like diphtheria, polio, typhoid fever, measles, and whooping cough, the second revolution was turning attention to public as well as private efforts in the home, the community, and the workplace to create environments that would prevent illness and promote good health.

One obstacle for those in public health, however, was that their work was rarely the sort of thing that made headlines or fired the public's imagination. Curative medicine had produced astonishing strides over the past several decades with the development of miracle drugs, organ transplantation, sophisticated diagnostic techniques, and other "magic bullet" procedures that captured public attention and drew government dollars. All but ignored, by comparison, were the more difficult and complex long-term solutions to problems of chronic disease, the area embraced by public health.

"The serious consequences of such priorities are now emerging," Dean Henderson wrote in the Fall 1984 issue of *In Brief,* the School's quarterly newsletter: "In the past 20 years, expenditures for health care have quadrupled. Today, more than ten cents of every dollar is spent for health care and the costs are rising....Yet for all that has been and is being spent, the results in terms of longevity or quality of life have been far less than anticipated.

"We can expect, for example, a far larger proportion of elderly in our society and an even greater demand for curative and rehabilitative services. Costs inevitably will continue to escalate, but even now, we face a major crisis in funding for our tax-supported insurance programs. Of no less concern is a proliferating array of new chemicals whose risks are largely unknown....Alcohol and drug abuse also is a growing problem, as yet without solution. Finally, the world's population problem unless vigorously addressed, promises starvation, global insecurity and migration of unprecedented proportions."

Public health professionals alone could not solve these problems, Dean Henderson said, but fundamental to any possible solution was an understanding of how and why diseases occur and how they could be prevented. Of equal importance was the promotion of behavior and life-styles which sustained good health, and the restructuring of a health care system of acceptable quality which all could afford. It was to those ends that he sought to apply the School's resources to the best advantage. The result was an elaboration of programs in three basic areas: environmental science, health policy and management, and international health.

In the Department of Environmental Health Sciences, the School developed a broad-based program which extended from basic research out into the workplace to tackle specific current problems, and which was unique among schools of public health. Under the chairmanship of Gareth M. Green, the department investigated a wide range of environmental and occupational hazards. A Center for Occupational and Environmental Health was established with the School of Medicine, which became a valuable resource to industry, labor, and government. An Associates Program for Industry and Labor was set up, and the Industrial Council for Tropical Health chose the School as its resource center. Dr. Green was among the first American scientists sent by the Centers for Disease Control in Atlanta to Bhopal, India, in December 1984, following an accidental release of deadly gas from a chemical plant that killed thousands of nearby residents. On his return, he led a symposium that dealt with the risks of transporting hazardous chemicals through populated areas and the limited ability of medical facilities to respond to major chemical disasters.

A reconstituted Department of Health Policy and Management was headed by Karen Davis, former deputy assistant secretary of health in the Carter administration. Among its principal areas of investigation were the crucial areas of health care costs, access to health care for the aged and underprivileged, and the financing of health care. This was also a unique operation among American schools of public health. A Center for Hospital Finance and Management within the department began playing a national role in developing procedures to help hospitals improve management and restrain costs. Another innovative activity was the Health Program Alliance, designed to foster mutually beneficial relationships between faculty and students and health agencies in Maryland and surrounding states by assisting those agencies with specific problems; the program was a prototype for a congressional initiative to establish centers for health promotion and disease prevention across the country. A Health Services Research and Development Center, which had been established in 1971, emerged as one of the foremost organizations of its type in the country. In 1981,

The worldwide impact of the School of Hygiene and Public Health is exemplified in the work of Alfred Sommer, holder of a joint appointment in the School and the Wilmer Institute, who studied the effectiveness of vitamin A supplements in preventing blindness among Indonesian children.

the nation's first Program for Control of Childhood Injuries—which were taking the lives of 10,000 children a year nationally—was founded as a joint venture with the School of Medicine.

In the field of international health, a new Institute for International Health Programs was established in 1984 under the leadership of W. Henry Mosley, professor of population dynamics, who had returned to the School after seven years of work in India and Africa. Also unique among schools of public health, the institute was designed to serve as an academic base for international health programs in developing countries and to coordinate the efforts of about 60 faculty members working in that area. Another basic part of the School's international health program dealt with industrialized countries. In 1980, the School was designated by the World Health Organization as its only collaborating center in the United States for the study of health problems of industrialized countries, encompassing such areas as accident prevention, alcoholism, and occupational medicine. In 1980, the School joined with the Wilmer Eye Institute to establish a new International Center for Epidemiology and Preventive Ophthalmology as part of the World Health Organization's effort to wipe out eye diseases caused by infection, poor nutrition, or inadequate public health measures. It was the most comprehensive blindness prevention campaign ever mounted.

* * *

In addition to these three areas of rapid growth, the School continued to develop its teaching and research capabilities in more traditional sectors of public health, such as epidemiology, biostatistics, health education, maternal and child health, and behavioral sciences. Major research contributions in the early 1980s included dramatic progress in development of a male contraceptive and in schistosomiasis control.

The principal master's degree program, the Master of Public Health, in 1982 was reformulated and extended from nine to 11 months, a move that other schools quickly copied. The doctoral program remained strong, as indicated by the fact that nearly 20 percent of all doctorates conferred by schools of public health were being given by Johns Hopkins. A part-time master's program was approved, and the School's continuing education program was expanded. Residency programs in preventive medicine and occupational medicine were greatly strengthened and came to rank as the country's largest and best known. The Department of Mental Hygiene continued to be the only such unit in an American school of public health; one of its unique efforts was a program of preventive intervention among young Baltimore school children who displayed overly-aggressive or anxious personalities.

Johns Hopkins' preeminence in the field of population studies continued to be enhanced by work in the Department of Population Dynamics and its Population Center, which encompassed programs ranging from basic research in reproductive biology to the implementation of family-planning programs in developed and under-developed countries. The department's Population Information Program, funded by the U.S. Agency for International Development, prepared multi-language editions of six reports each year dealing with topical subjects in family planning and related issues.

* * *

The field of public health in the early 1980s demonstrated perhaps better than any other major Hopkins activity the swelling current of interdisciplinary studies at the University. It was an area where "intellectual hybrids" truly flourished. These were investigators who were firmly based in one or more of the major disciplines but were capable of integrating knowledge and skills from several different areas. More and more, problems in the public health field required contributions from professionals in many widely diverse fields— physicians, economists, engineers, ethicists, behavioral scientists, management experts, as well as those engaged in basic science research.

This led to the forging of many ties between the School of Hygiene and Public Health and other Hopkins divisions, including an unlikely alliance with the Peabody Institute in the area of environmental sound studies, and those that have already been mentioned between medicine, engineering, and other disciplines. Some of the School's work also necessitated collaboration with specialists not found within the Hopkins galaxy. Lawyers were needed to advise on the mountain of new regulatory laws that had been passed to deal with environmental disasters like Love Canal, dangerous materials such as asbestos, automotive safety, power plant radiation, and other recently recognized hazards. Links were developed with private industry to a degree unseen in the past, as industrial leaders came to appreciate more fully their responsibilities for the health and well being of both the employee and the community in which they operated.

* * *

Just as the areas in which it worked changed dramatically in the 1970s and early 1980s, the School experienced a major shift in its support base which reflected changing economic and political conditions. The total value of the School's outside funding grew from $16.1 million to $37.7 million between 1974 and 1984, but the sources of that support were markedly different at the end of the period than at the beginning.

The federal share dropped suddenly and sharply under the Reagan administration, as substantial training funds which had supported both students and faculty in health services research and public health were discontinued. The changes were so abrupt that the School experienced a serious deficit problem for several years before it was able to readjust, even though efforts had begun in the late 1970s to broaden the support base. Those efforts centered on increased work with the private sector in the form of both grants and contracts with industry and labor.

By 1983, a turnaround in the support picture had become apparent. While revenues from federal sources declined by $3 million from the preceding year, private support—which had never exceeded $3 million altogether until 1982— jumped in one year from $3.7 to $7.7 million. Efforts were also made to enlarge the School's relatively small endowment—$28.2 million, compared with $135.7 million for the School of Medicine and $71.2 million for the School of Arts and Sciences. The School had only two endowed chairs.

Another global change in the School's character was in the size of its student body, which increased from 480 in 1971 to nearly 900 in 1985, with members from most states and more than 50 foreign countries. Doctoral and postdoctoral candidates constituted about half the student population, which was equally divided between men and women. The faculty numbered 294 full-time and 210 part-time members, representing all major biomedical and social science disciplines. Alumni continued to find their way into deanships and faculty appointments at other schools of public health, into leadership positions in health agencies of the U.S. government, and into influential positions in the public health sector abroad.

* * *

Among schools of public health worldwide, the Hopkins institution in the 1980s was by any measure the largest and most prestigious, with 100 more full-time faculty than the second largest school, the University of North Carolina. Among the divisions of Johns Hopkins, the School also stood out, but almost as an anomaly. It was not of the "small but beautiful" genre that had traditionally marked Hopkins academic divisions. It was a big operation in its own right, and the only academic unit of the University that stood as the largest among its world peers in terms of physical size and impact—by sheer weight of its research program and the contribution of its alumni—on its area of specialization.

SAIS—a look to the East

From its philosophical beginnings in Germanic educational tradition, the international character of Johns Hopkins found expression over the years through the activities of virtually all of its academic divisions. It is not surprising, then, that the centerpiece of the institution's global outlook—the School of Advanced International Studies—served as a forward unit when the international character of the University began to broaden dramatically in the late 1970s.

The School had benefited considerably from the Hopkins Hundreds campaign in the form of three new endowed chairs, although it remained underendowed when compared with some of its peer institutions. The campaign also produced heartening support from alumni. Major contributions from private foundations and other organizations—on which the School had always been critically dependent—also showed a marked increase. Some of that funding supported further development of Middle Eastern studies, Asian studies, and the Center of Canadian Studies.

183

In 1978, the School opened a new Center of Brazilian Studies, supported by private business interests in Brazil and the United States. It was the first American organization devoted to the study of Brazilian foreign relations and policies, and was organized in response to Brazil's emergence as one of the most important of the new middle-range states.

'... it is time to look toward East Asia because academic interests, science, trade, and diplomacy are focusing more intensely on that region. A great university needs to be part of that.'

Richard P. Longaker

Enrollments continued to rise in the late 1970s, to the point where facilities were taxed to the limit. A growing alumni population began to have an increasing impact in international relations and politics. In one year, seven SAIS graduates were serving as U.S. or foreign ambassadors to other countries. When President Carter was deeply involved in negotiations between Egypt and Israel, both American ambassadors to those countries were SAIS alumni. Bologna Center alumni had won seats in the parliaments of Britain and France and, in 1976, James A. Leach, an Iowa Republican, became the first SAIS graduate elected to the U.S. Congress.

* * *

In 1979, Robert Osgood stepped down after six years as dean and returned to teaching and policy research at the

Dean George R. Packard of the School of Advanced International Studies, left, is shown with Benjamin T. Rome, a 1925 alumnus and major supporter of SAIS's expanded program of Asian studies. Mr. Rome was awarded an honorary doctorate by the University in 1982.

School. He was succeeded by George R. Packard, former deputy director of the Woodrow Wilson International Center for Scholars, former executive editor of the *Philadelphia Bulletin,* and a highly regarded specialist in Asian and Pacific affairs.

By coincidence, the same year Dr. Packard assumed the deanship, U.S. trade with Asian nations for the first time exceeded trade with Europe, and scholars began talking of a shift of world energy to the Pacific basin. SAIS had begun moving toward greater Asian involvement several years before, but under Dean Packard, that movement quickened. A major boost came in 1980 with a $1 million gift from the George and Sadie Hyman Foundation to establish a professorship in Chinese studies. At a reception announcing the gift, President Muller reported on the start of a new cooperative program between Johns Hopkins and the University of Nanjing; guests enjoyed sesame chicken and plum wine as the first Peabody Conservatory students from the People's Republic of China performed in the background.

The niceties of the occasion were appropriate, for it was the forerunner of a formal agreement to establish the first U.S.-China joint educational enterprise since resumption of diplomatic relations between the two countries. Known as the Hopkins-Nanjing Center for Chinese and American Studies, the facility was to be a cooperative venture for American and Chinese graduate students in the history, politics, economics, international relations, and other aspects of the two great powers. Ground was broken in 1984 for a 64,000-square-foot building for the Center, which was constructed by the Chinese and administered by SAIS. Commented Johns Hopkins Provost Richard P. Longaker on the occasion: "Our school in Bologna, Italy, sets a precedent for the Hopkins-Nanjing Center. Having established ourselves firmly in Europe, it is time to look toward East Asia because academic interests, science, trade, and diplomacy are focusing more intensely on that region. A great university needs to be part of that."

* * *

While Johns Hopkins' ties with China go back to the early

1900s when William H. Welch assisted in setting up Peking Union Medical College, the University's association with Japan is even older. In the late 19th century, many Japanese students in the Meiji Restoration sought advanced education in the United States. Of the 39 Ph.D.s awarded to foreign nationals at Hopkins between 1876 and 1901, ten went to Japanese. One of these was Inazo Nitobe, a prominent educator and statesman who became a close friend of classmate Woodrow Wilson.

In 1982, the U.S.-Japan Foundation in New York made a grant of $150,000 for the establishment of a U.S.-Japan Study Center at SAIS. This stimulus fed the already-growing appetite for Far Eastern studies at the School. The following May, Japanese Prime Minister Yasuhiro Nakasone accepted an invitation to deliver the commencement address at SAIS. He spoke in English, the first Japanese prime minister to do so at such an event. Students, speaking in Japanese, took the occasion to present the Japanese leader with a SAIS T-shirt and a birthday cake, which he graciously accepted.

In 1984, President Muller led a Johns Hopkins delegation to Japan which had momentous consequences. As Suzuki violinists played Mozart and the Johns Hopkins seal hung

Prominent Japanese educator and statesman Inazo Nitobe studied at Johns Hopkins at the same time as Woodrow Wilson and became his close friend. On a 1984 trip to Japan, President Steven Muller planted two Maryland dogwood trees at Nitobe's birthplace to honor this distinguished alumnus, who is also memorialized on Japanese currency.

above the stage in Tokyo's Hotel Okura, Dr. Muller bestowed an honorary degree upon Prime Minister Nakasone—the first degree that Hopkins had ever awarded off campus, let alone in another country.

At the same time, Dr. Muller and Dean Packard announced the establishment of the Edwin O. Reischauer Center for East Asian Studies at SAIS, which would consolidate programs on China, Japan, and Southeast Asia and attempt to broaden the exchange of scholars. The Center was named for the former American ambassador to Japan who, in the 1960s, was highly regarded in both countries for his work in repairing the "broken dialogue" between them.

During the trip, the Hopkins group traveled to Morioka in northern Japan, the birthplace of Nitobe, to plant two dogwood trees brought 10,000 miles from Maryland at a statue honoring this distinguished alumnus and one of Japan's most visionary citizens.

* * *

Increased attention to the Far East did not diminish the interest of SAIS faculty and students in other areas of the world. In addition to the new Hyman chair, three others were funded—in Middle East Studies, African Studies, and International Finance and Economics. The last was partly in response to a historic shift that began taking place at the School in the mid-1970s. Whereas SAIS had been founded primarily to train foreign service officers and others in government, by 1985 about half its graduates were going into private sector jobs in such fields as international banking, corporate management, and journalism.

Curriculum changes were made to accommodate the new interest pattern, but the interdisciplinary approach to the study of international relations that had always been a distinguishing characteristic of the School was maintained. Joint degree programs were established with the Wharton School of the University of Pennsylvania, leading to M.B.A./M.S. degrees, and with the Stanford University Law School, leading to J.D/M.A. degrees. An executive-in-residence program was set up, making available to SAIS students the experience of a leading corporate executive for counseling in corporate matters. All this did not mean that SAIS was becoming a business school, however, Dean Packard emphasized in the Winter 1985 issue of *SAISPHERE,* the School's semiannual magazine. "We still insist on a strong concentration in international economics, a mastery of at least one foreign language, and a broad knowledge of history and international relations," he said.

As evidence, he pointed to the core curriculum adopted by the faculty in 1979. It required that all students pass examinations in three out of four core areas: history, American foreign policy, comparative national systems, and theories of the international economic and political system. As an added underpinning to students' preparation, the School increased emphasis on getting its young people into the field to test their language skills and to experience first-hand the areas in which they were especially interested. Jordan, Brazil, Japan, Kenya, Argentina, and Mexico are among countries in which SAIS students are able to spend time.

* * *

Another major development was the establishment in 1980 of the Johns Hopkins Foreign Policy Institute, a research and publications center involving the entire SAIS faculty and guest experts in diplomacy, business, the communications media, politics, government, and education. Roundtables and informal discussions of major aspects of international relations and American foreign policy produced what some observers characterized as some of Washington's most fascinating dialogue. The Institute also revived the semiannual *SAIS Review,* which was edited by students and published articles by such authorities as Defense Secretary Caspar Weinberger, Senators Dale Bumpers, John Glenn, and Charles McC. Mathias Jr., and numerous SAIS faculty. The Institute was opened under the chairmanship of former U.S. ambassador and Middle East expert Lucius D. Battle, who was succeeded in 1984 by former Secretary of Defense Harold Brown.

The Institute reinforced the growing perception of SAIS as another Washington "think tank," like the Brookings Institution located directly across Massachusetts Avenue. In a 1985 interview, Dean Packard said he did not mind such association, but stressed that the primary business of SAIS was educating students, not serving government and corporations with research studies and policy papers. However, the popular identification of SAIS was a matter of some concern to him, he said, recalling his effort soon after becoming dean to get a more identifiable name for the School to replace what to some was a rather meaningless acronym. The alumni would have none of this, Dean Packard said, so he began encouraging faculty to write more "op-ed page" articles and appear on programs like the *MacNeil/Lehrer Newshour*. Effort was also put into taking greater advantage of the School's location in the nation's capital by involving lawmakers, members of the executive branch, and officers of international organizations based in Washington in the School's programs and activities.

An organization as complex and wide ranging as the School of Advanced International Studies has many facets that can only be mentioned here. Italian President Sandro Pertini visited the School in 1982, accepted an award, dispensed with his prepared speech, and mingled for 45 minutes with students crammed into the student lounge. Before President Reagan's 1983 visit to Japan, SAIS convened a group of experts to brief the press on U.S.-Japan relations. The School in 1985 appointed former ambassador to Israel Samuel Lewis, a 1954 alumnus, as its diplomat-in-residence. The 1985 graduating class contained students from 50 countries from Austria to Zimbabwe (none as yet from the Soviet Union), from 33 U.S. states, representing 153 universities. The School had alumni chapters throughout the United States and in such countries as Brazil, Japan, China, and Saudi Arabia. In cooperation with the Johns Hopkins School of Hygiene and Public Health, SAIS instituted a dual M.A/M.H.S. degree to prepare students for careers that required health care knowledge as well as an understanding of international political, socioeconomic, and cultural issues.

* * *

SAIS's European outpost, the Center for European Studies in Bologna, Italy, continued to offer American and European graduate students the opportunity to study together under an international faculty in the oldest learning center in the western world. Funding, however, became a major problem in the mid-1970s when a five-year grant from the Italian government expired. The U.S. Agency for International Development continued its support, but even that was vulnerable to the winds of political change in Washington. Solvency for the Bologna Center was the chief concern of Wilfrid L. Kohl when he became the Center's third director in 1976, and it continued to be a high priority for his successors, Ronald Tiersky, who took over in 1980, and Robert G. Gard, former president of the National Defense University, who was appointed director in 1982.

Through new grants for research and conferences, fellowship donations, and support from additional European countries—including Germany and Great Britain—the Center not only survived but flourished. The quality of its research became increasingly recognized as its scholars explored such issues as the European monetary system, energy policies in Europe and America, inflation, and the Atlantic

In 1955, the School of Advanced International Studies established a center in Bologna, Italy, the first American graduate school in Europe for the study of international relations. The Center occupied this modern building in 1961.

alliance. The curriculum was broadened to focus more on general international relations with not only the United States but the rest of the world. In the spring of 1984, President Muller and a small group of Bologna students and faculty were granted a private audience with Pope John Paul II, who praised the Center's educational goals.

By its 30th anniversary in 1985, the Bologna Center had graduated some 2,400 students, most of whom had found positions in multinational corporations, international diplomacy, or universities throughout the world. During ceremonies marking that anniversary, President Pertini was presented with an honorary degree by the University, a fitting climax to 30 years of unique contributions to international education by the Italy-based school.

191

Peabody's instant new dimension

The story of how Johns Hopkins University came to affiliate with Baltimore's Peabody Institute, one of the nation's leading music schools, is not just the account of an interesting institutional marriage but an example of how a unique response to changing conditions in economics and education resulted in unexpected benefits to both parties.

Outwardly, the two institutions were vastly different, at least as far as their products were concerned. Where Hopkins turned out professionals in science, the humanities, medicine, engineering, and education, Peabody turned out professionals in the composition, performance, conducting, and teaching of music. Scores of Peabody alumni played as members of major symphony orchestras, taught at conservatories around the world, and administered leading schools and musical organizations. Thousands of nonprofessionals received instruction in instruments, voice, and dance for personal enrichment through the Preparatory Department, known to generations of Baltimoreans as "The Prep." Some Peabody alumni were among the lucky few who won fame and fortune in music— opera stars James Morris and Veronica Tyler, pianists Andre Watts and Ann Schein, composers Dominick Argento and Hugo Weisgall, organist Virgil Fox, and saxophonist-*cum*-Johnny Carson foil on NBC's *Tonight Show,* Tommy Newsom.

'Here we have an opportunity with the conjunction of a major school of music and a world-renowned research university of doing things ... in ways that no independent school of music could ever do.'

Robert Pierce

Peabody was founded in 1857, nearly 20 years before the University, by George Foster Peabody, a wealthy businessman and philanthropist who sought to enhance the cultural life of Baltimore, the city in which he had grown up. He endowed an institute with

Wealthy businessman George Foster Peabody founded the Peabody Institute in 1857 as a means to enhance the cultural life of Baltimore. His philanthropic nature is believed to have influenced Johns Hopkins, of whom Peabody was a good friend, as well as such other Baltimore benefactors as Enoch Pratt and Henry Walters.

four main functions: a library, art gallery, lecture series, and a conservatory of music. While the library was the first of this diffuse set of functions to open, the mission most clearly defined by history was that of the conservatory. It was the country's first major music school in concept, although not the first to open, the result of construction delays during the Civil War. When Peabody's building was formally dedicated in October 1866, the occasion marked the first time in five years that many of the trustees spoke to each other, as their sympathies had been almost evenly divided between the Union and the Confederacy.

Once in operation, the Conservatory quickly established itself as the country's foremost producer of musicians, performers, and composers, a position it held well into the 20th century. The school also contributed a number of distinctive academic innovations. Though cast in the European mold of an elite trade school for the training of a gifted minority who would display their talents for a few aristocratic patrons, as Peabody evolved in Baltimore this model changed. Marking an early commitment to the highest level of professionalism, the Conservatory introduced graduate study in music. Almost from the outset, it offered a variety of musical programs that the general public was encouraged to attend. In 1898, it established the Preparatory Division, one of the earliest efforts by any school to bring knowledge and appreciation of music to the widest possible spectrum of the population. Peabody was thus one of the first conservatories to generate consumers as well as performers of music.

In terms of its physical plant, Peabody was blessed with several of what were to become some of the most historically and esthetically valuable buildings in downtown Baltimore. Located on Mount Vernon Place, site of Baltimore's historic Washington Monument, Peabody took its position among the city's architectural jewels of the period. The setting nurtured a basic philosophy that stressed a carefully chosen student body, a small faculty of international repute, and an obligation not only to music but to the community in which the institution functioned.

In the early 1920s, the nature of music education in the United States began to change, as did the hierarchy of institutions that provided it. While Peabody had long enjoyed the largest endowment of any school of its kind (about $13 million in 1930), the fortunes of philanthropists like Eastman, Curtis, and Juilliard established schools with at least twice Peabody's endowment. The result was predictable—with much more money, the newer schools were able to recruit the best faculty and attract the best students, and Peabody's preeminence began to fade. It was not helped by another development in music education after World War II—the explosion of public higher education which added a completely new tier of quality professional music schools.

These events conspired to bring Peabody to a desperate financial situation in the mid-1970s. The training of musicians was one of the most expensive forms of education, requiring a substantial component of individual instruction and a student-faculty ratio, in Peabody's case, of one faculty member for each five students. Nor was this type of education susceptible to such modern remedies as audio-visual aids and computer technology. As inflation took ever-deepening bites in purchasing power, the Institute was forced to spend endowment funds to close the gap between income and operating costs. Those funds were heading for exhaustion by the end of the decade, and it was obvious that if Peabody were to continue functioning, major restructuring and refinancing were necessary.

* * *

Out of a process of intense self-examination and planning, Peabody's strategy for survival was drawn. As it turned out, circumstances were right to take a noteworthy step in American musical education. In the most sweeping organizational change in its history, Peabody entered into an affiliation with Johns Hopkins University. It was an idea that had been advanced several times in the past, but, in 1977, after careful new consideration, the trustees of both institutions concluded that the idea's time had come and that a formal affiliation was in the best interests of both parties.

There was ample justification for such a step in the histories of both institutions. George Peabody and Johns Hopkins had been good friends, with Peabody once reportedly having

Peabody's main building was dedicated in 1866 and is located on Mount Vernon Square in downtown Baltimore. One of the nation's earliest and best known schools of music, Peabody affiliated with Johns Hopkins in 1977.

told Hopkins that he was "the only man I have met in all my experience more thoroughly anxious to make money and more determined to succeed than myself." Peabody also described his plans for the Institute and told Hopkins of the great satisfaction that was to be found in giving money for "good and humane purposes." Peabody is believed to have strongly influenced Hopkins and other Baltimoreans, including Henry Walters and Enoch Pratt, to follow his example.

There were many connections between the two institutions from the earliest days. The original Howard Street location of Johns Hopkins University was chosen because Hopkins had no library of its own, but relied on the nearby Peabody library to serve its faculty and students. (An ironic cycling of history brought the 250,000-volume Peabody library into the custody of Hopkins 106 years later in 1982, following a 17-year stewardship by Baltimore's Enoch Pratt library system.) The Peabody Orchestra played at the inauguration of Daniel Coit Gilman, and Peabody's first summer session in 1912 was sponsored jointly with the University. In 1931, a bachelor of science degree was offered by Peabody through Hopkins. Over the years, students and faculty of the institutions enjoyed an informal program of cultural exchange that grew out of mutual complementarity.

For Johns Hopkins, the affiliation meant an instant new dimension in its liberal arts resources and the coupling of a name and reputation that was congruent with its own. For Peabody, it represented access to highly advanced administrative machinery as well as a fund-raising apparatus that had just been finely tuned through the University's Hopkins Hundreds campaign. At the same time, the agreement guaranteed Peabody's corporate identity, academic autonomy, and fiscal responsibility. Both institutions shared in the enriching cross-fertilization that inevitably accompanied increased traffic between the two campuses.

If the affiliation between a conservatory of music and a research-oriented university had implications for the future of other private educational enterprises, so did a second distinctive development in Peabody's postaffiliation history. Peabody planned a major capital campaign, but this took time to organize and even longer to produce results. An appeal was made to the State of Maryland for public assistance that was unprecedented in terms and magnitude for an independent education institution. But the request was approved and the Maryland General Assembly voted to provide Peabody with $2.7 million in aid over a three-year period.

The state later committed itself to contributing $900,000 a year for 12 years, conditional on Peabody's raising $1 million a year for its endowment through that period. This demonstration of official faith in Peabody assured that the continuity of the institution was not in jeopardy. It also gave the trustees breathing space to plan and develop a combination of private and public support that was emerging as the most promising pathway to long-term successful operation. At no time during these deliberations was it seriously suggested that the state take over Peabody (as it recently had another small private university in Baltimore), recognition that such a highly specialized operation as Peabody's would flourish best in the private sector.

* * *

To go with its new structure, Peabody appointed a new administration. Chosen as director was Elliott W. Galkin, a graduate of the Paris Conservatory, Ecole Normale, Academy of Music in Vienna, and Cornell University. He had also served as chairman of the music department at Goucher College and music critic for the Baltimore *Sun*. Also named were a new academic dean, a dean of students, a director of development, and a business manager. The board of trustees, under chairman Richard W. Case, was enlarged and strengthened.

Changes in emphasis were made in the curriculum under Dr. Galkin, who was an enthusiastic champion of America's musical heritage and who believed that the Conservatory should recognize its debt to American composers as well as its European heritage. Music by American composers was included in all performances by Peabody groups, a lecture series on "Music in American Life" was established, and the Conservatory's first quartet-in-residence was established and named the American String Quartet. Dr. Galkin also saw the modern conservatory as deriving much of its vitality from the community it served, and stepped up the schedule of public concerts—such as a performance by the Peabody Symphony Orchestra at the Baltimore Orioles' opening game in 1980—and the activities of the Preparatory Department.

Among new academic programs that were developed following the affiliation was a graduate program in conducting, an area that had been almost totally neglected by American schools of music. Another new program, the first of its kind in this country, was a Master of Music History and Criticism, which made use of Peabody's new access to the nationally known creative writing program at Hopkins.

To restore its financial solidity, Peabody in 1980 launched a $12 million capital campaign, seeking $7.5 million in new endowment, $2.5 million for renovation of its concert hall, and $2 million for operating support. The campaign goal was met in less than five years, aided by 25 contributions of $100,000 or more. The largest single gift was $1 million toward the concert hall renovation from trustee Sidney M. Friedberg in memory of his wife, Miriam, whom he had met when both were studying piano at Peabody; the concert hall was named in her honor. Peabody immediately embarked on a second phase of its fund-raising effort as part of a major new campaign that was being inaugurated by Johns Hopkins. Peabody hoped to raise an additional $25 million in this phase, which was to continue through February 1990.

Dr. Galkin stepped down as director in 1983. After a national search for a successor, a special committee decided that the best person to handle the job was already on the staff, former dean and acting director Robert Pierce. A graduate of the New England Conservatory of Music and best known locally as principal horn of the Baltimore Symphony Orchestra, Pierce had been a Peabody faculty member since 1958. He appointed Eileen T. Cline, former director of the Neighborhood Music School in New Haven, Connecticut, as dean.

One of the new director's first undertakings was to initiate a major self-study of the institution in order to formulate goals for its future development. A leading priority was to accelerate the task of restoring Peabody's reputation as one of America's best music schools. The crucial ingredient was an increase in faculty salaries, not only to draw the best people to Peabody but to protect against faculty raiding by other schools.

Beyond that, Pierce said in an interview in *Peabody News*, the school's monthly newspaper, soon after being named director, "Peabody was founded as an institution that was very avant-garde for its time and we now need to recapture that sense of adventure and chart new courses." In a later interview, he said: "Because we are now merged with Johns Hopkins, we ought to be more than just one of the major music schools in the country. We ought to be in the forefront of charting new courses, new directions, furthering the boundaries of music through the establishing of interdisciplinary activities. Here we have an opportunity with the conjunction of a major school of music and a world-renowned research university of doing things in the field of combining music and technology, music and science, music and the humanities—in ways that no independent school of music could ever do."

A program that was already in place by 1984 served as an example, the Bachelor of Music in Recording Arts and Sciences. It was a five-year program in audio engineering that combined the resources of Peabody in music with those of Hopkins' G.W.C. Whiting School of Engineering in electrical engineering and computer science. To accommodate the program and other recording needs, Peabody constructed a new recording studio complex that featured the latest in sound engineering technology and sound reinforcement facilities, including equipment for analog/digital music synthesis.

* * *

As the Peabody-Hopkins affiliation entered its seventh year in 1983, *Peabody News* published appraisals by two of the men most deeply involved in the venture. Peabody trustees' chairman Richard Case said: "The affiliation provided an administrative framework, but it is the people in both institutions who have made it creative. What none of us could predict at the time was that only six years after the affiliation, some Peabody students would be taking electrical engineering courses at the G.W.C. Whiting School of Engineering, or that a Peabody composer would be sharing his researches with colleagues at the Kennedy Institute for Handicapped Children."

President Steven Muller said: "I can reflect only that the decision for Peabody and Hopkins to affiliate was appropriate at the time. The synergism that we spoke of with hope in the 1970s came into being naturally, and perhaps the best augury for the future is that I have not heard anyone suggest that the two institutions should ever separate. What has resulted is indeed greater than the sum of the parts."

An impartial view of the importance to music and to Johns Hopkins of Peabody's continued healthy functioning may be found in a February 12, 1985, editorial in the Baltimore *Sun*. Commenting on the success of the $12 million capital campaign, the editorial said: "The Peabody is not just a local institution. It provides musicians and teachers to the world and nation. It is a great asset to Maryland, from which it

The Peabody-Hopkins Chorus frequently joins the Peabody Symphony Orchestra in public performances. Affiliation between Peabody and Johns Hopkins enhanced the cultural opportunities afforded by both venerable Baltimore institutions.

receives and still needs $900,000 a year; to Baltimore, where it greatly enriches the musical life in countless ways; and to the university, to which it brings an eminence in one-on-one teaching and in a very lively art to relieve the science-medicine-defense-research strengths that overcontribute to the Hopkins reputation."

* * *

In the fall of 1985, Johns Hopkins and Peabody strengthened their affiliation with a new agreement. A withdrawal clause in the original agreement which permitted either institution to break the affiliation with a year's notice was eliminated, and the University assumed full fiscal responsibility for the Institute in return for its physical assets. "The new agreement makes the affiliation between the two institutions permanent," Dr. Muller said in announcing the change, which was approved by both boards of trustees. He stressed that it was not a merger, since the Peabody corporation would continue with a new board responsible for the Institute's endowment and art collection. Henry R. Lord, who became chairman of the existing Peabody board upon the death of Mr. Case in 1984, said the new agreement was the natural result of the success of the affiliation and expressed confidence that Peabody's academic and financial goals were thereby assured.

APL—unique capabilities

The officially stated mission of the Applied Physics Laboratory from its beginning was "the application of science and technology to the enhancement of national security and other human needs to which its facilities can make an especially favorable contribution." Despite an undercurrent of anti-military feeling that grew among many students and some faculty in the wake of American involvement in Vietnam, the position of the University and its trustees continued to be that APL was serving a vital national need and represented a major commitment to public service by Johns Hopkins in the area of national security.

The main work at APL was related originally to the defense needs of the U.S. Navy's surface fleet, and later to submarines. APL, in fact, became by far the largest of the Navy-affiliated university laboratories. The military aspect of APL's work was, of course, partially closed to public discussion. Several points are worth noting, however. APL was a "full spectrum" facility, in the sense that it engaged in a range of research and engineering activities from basic research and exploratory development, through design, systems engineering, prototype development and fabrication, to test and demonstration. The staff in the early 1980s consisted of nearly 1,500

In carrying out its defense mission, APL developed unique capabilities that proved to be directly transferable to a variety of non-military applications.

scientists and engineers, of whom 240 held doctorates and 600 held master's degrees. Physical facilities included almost 40 specialized engineering and testing laboratories working in energy conversion and propulsion, combat systems and radar development, missile guidance and control, acoustic signal processing, spacecraft systems assembly and testing, computer and data processing, and other specialties. In addition, there were 20 basic research laboratories in the Milton S. Eisenhower Research Center.

In carrying out its defense mission, APL developed unique capabilities that proved to be directly transferable to a variety of non-military applications. In 1984, about 15 percent of its activities were non-defense related. These took the forms of research and development in the area of space technology and of increasing cooperative research with the academic divisions of the University in biomedical engineering, energy research, computer-aided instruction, environmental studies, oceanography, and basic research in physics, chemistry, and mathematics.

In space, APL in 1985 marked a quarter century of outstanding work in satellite design and construction. The first Hopkins-built spacecraft, the Transit 1B, which was launched in 1960, marked the beginning of the Navy Navigational Satellite System and opened the door for worldwide, all-weather precision navigation that enabled not only Navy ships but commercial and private vessels down to the size of small yachts to determine their position at sea to within a tenth of a mile.

In 1977, the Laboratory began work on a new NASA orbiter designed to study the magnetosphere and moons of Jupiter. In the following year, APL developed a radar altimeter for SEASAT, the first satellite designed specifically for research on the world's oceans; the altimeter was able to measure sea levels to an accuracy of 10 centimeters. The APL-built satellite, MAGSAT, was launched by NASA in 1980 to make precision mappings of the earth's magnetic field.

When the Voyager satellites swept by Saturn in 1981, APL instruments on board found unusual properties in the giant planet's magnetosphere. In 1983, HILAT, a Navy navigation satellite modified at APL, made the first daylight photographs in the upper atmosphere of the aurora borealis. A unique three-satellite experiment in space physics was conducted in 1984 using an APL-built satellite and two others constructed in Great Britain and West Germany. The three satellites in different orbits were used to study the interaction of the solar wind with the earth's magnetic field, and over the Pacific Ocean on December 27, 1984, they analyzed the first man-made "comet," ionized gas that was injected into the upper atmosphere to interact with the solar wind.

In March 1985, a new APL-developed GEOSAT ocean surveying satellite was launched with the capability of measuring ocean contours and surveying the worldwide gravitational field at the ocean's surface with greater precision than was possible before. The GEOSAT was the 50th APL-developed satellite launched since Transit 1B.

* * *

Energy researchers at APL pioneered the dramatic ocean thermal energy concept of using temperature differences between warm, upper layers of tropical oceans and cooler, bottom layers to generate electricity. Other scientists devel-

The Applied Physics Laboratory began developing this major facility in Howard County, Maryland, in 1954. Now one of the country's largest university-affiliated research centers, APL does defense-related work for the U.S. Navy, as well as space research, satellite development, biomedical engineering, alternative energy source investigations, and other non-military studies.

oped plans for the productive use of underground sources of hot water and brines that were found in many areas of the country. Another concept investigated was the possibility of using water reservoirs near cities to store heat removed from buildings in summer for use the following winter. APL also was a leader in developing advanced flywheel technology as a system of energy storage that could be used by utilities and vehicles to ease the burden of peak power demands.

Other important research was done on improved traffic control systems for ocean terminals and airports and on the causes of clear air turbulence that posed a threat to aircraft safety. Another study sought to understand and predict the occurrence of massive ocean waves before they endangered ships, oil rigs, or coastal cities. An investigation of fatal residential fires in Maryland showed that 80 percent of the deaths were caused not by burns but by victims' inhaling toxic gases, often from burning plastic. APL even helped the U.S. Fish and Wildlife Service track large migratory birds by building a 5.7-ounce transmitter that could be attached to a bird and send signals that were picked up by orbiting satellites.

* * *

The area of medicine provided some of the most striking examples of research in which APL collaborated with other divisions of the University. Development continued on the externally powered and controlled prosthetic devices for amputees that had begun in the late 1960s. A new electrically powered wheelchair was designed with greatly improved maneuverability and control. In 1981, Hopkins neurosurgeons implanted a new tissue stimulator that electronically relieved intractable pain in a patient who had suffered continuously since an injury seven years before; known as the Neuropacemaker, the device used NASA technology and was developed under the leadership of Robert Fischell, who had previously produced the rechargeable heart pacemaker. He also developed a programmable implantable medication system which was designed to deliver precisely programmed amounts of medicine automatically to specified locations in the body. Other collaborative research between APL and the

Medical Institutions produced important instrumentation for studies of circulation in the eye and major arteries, and an implantable sensor for measuring intracranial pressure.

Joint research developed quickly and naturally between APL and the G.W.C. Whiting School of Engineering following its founding in 1979. Fields of mutual interest included materials science, non-destructive evaluation, computer-aided design and manufacturing, image processing, mathematical modeling and simulation, and robotics. Common interests between the School of Arts and Sciences and APL clearly existed in the field of oceanography; the former with its Chesapeake Bay Institute and the latter with its experience in physical oceanography, wave effects, remote sensing of surface and near surface phenomena, and numerical modeling of hydrodynamic fields.

* * *

The Applied Physics Laboratory had become a component of the part-time education enterprise at Hopkins in 1963, when it was designated as the first off-campus center of the Evening College. As it evolved, the APL Center's program focused on courses leading to M.S. degrees in electrical engineering, numerical science, applied physics, space technology, computer science, and technical management. Between 1968 and 1983, when responsibility for the APL program was transferred from the Evening College to the School of Engineering, nearly 1,600 Master of Science degrees were awarded to students at the APL Center.

* * *

Despite the segment of opinion that held that a university should not be involved with defense-related work, President Muller was unrestrained in response to an interviewer's question in the October 1979 *Johns Hopkins Magazine.* The question: "Intellectually, what do you find the most interesting area of Johns Hopkins?" Dr. Muller's answer:

"Many people won't like this, but I would have to say the Applied Physics Laboratory. You know almost 80 percent of what they do relates to national security. It's interesting, though, that when you talk to people from the Cousteau

Institute, they're deeply aware of Hopkins—mostly because APL is doing work on the problems of defending the nuclear fleet. Virtually everything APL is doing in this area is publishable and published research, because you have to know a great deal about the behavior of the ocean in order to work on how submarines behave in the ocean. When I last went to Germany, the Max Planck Association was acutely aware of Hopkins because of APL's work in space, and very little of that is classified. The stuff that we're doing in biomedical engineering is fantastic. . . . I will probably never persuade the people who have blinders on about anything that has to do with national defense, but I think of APL as an intellectual asset, not just a fiscal one—which it is only to a modest degree."

Computers come to campus

When asked by the *Johns Hopkins Magazine* in October 1983 to identify the greatest problem or opportunity facing the University, President Muller replied: "To recognize that we are in the middle of a revolution. That's a dramatic word, but in this case an unavoidable word, in speaking of the way in which this society produces, disseminates, and consumes information. Teaching institutions are directly exposed to fundamental changes in the way information is generated, disseminated, and absorbed. At a minimum we have to be up to date, and at a maximum try even to play some sort of leadership role."

The computer-communications revolution of which Dr. Muller spoke was indeed making a major impact on the conduct of both academic and administrative affairs at the University. The tasks of remaining up to date and aspiring to leadership in this field required large investments in new equipment as well as seldom-easy adjustments on the part of faculty and students to new ways of teaching, learning, and conducting research.

'We are in the middle of a revolution… an unavoidable word in speaking of the way in which this society produces, disseminates, and consumes information.'

Steven Muller

With little fanfare, a major advance in communications capability was activated at the University late in 1983. Two microwave dishes were placed atop Rowland Hall on the Homewood campus, one aimed at a sister dish on the roof of the Samuel W. Traylor Research Building on the medical campus, the other at a relay station atop Baltimore's tallest office building which provided line-of-sight linkage with the Applied Physics Laboratory in Howard County. The three campuses were thus joined by a private communications system that made possible the simultaneous transmission of voice, video, and digitized computer data. The greatest immediate benefit was a six-fold increase in the data transmission capacity of the University's computer network, previously dependent on slow and cumbersome telephone hook-ups. Another benefit was less expense—the University bought the hardware for $120,000, and operating costs were slight when weighed against the system's power and versatility.

This system was not the first use of microwave communication at the University. The Medical Institutions for several years had employed a microwave link that joined the School of Medicine, Francis Scott Key Medical Center, and Sinai Hospital to televise grand rounds among the three locations. An even earlier experimental project in medical imaging had allowed emergency room physicians at Hopkins Hospital and the Key Medical Center simultaneously to view and diagnose patients' X-rays.

The first use of the new microwave system that created a stir not only throughout the University but in the local press was the earlier-mentioned televised classes of the Whiting School of Engineering. The electronic transmission of part-time courses between Maryland Hall and the Kossiakoff Center at APL began during the 1984 spring term on a limited basis and was expanded to five regular courses that fall. From identical classrooms at each location, graduate-level students —seated two to a TV monitor/microphone-equipped table— watched and heard Homewood professors or APL staff scientists give lectures and illustrate points. By activating their microphones, students in either location were able to question and respond to the instructors. Professors reported interaction with the remote classes to be as lively as that in a regular classroom. Grades in the "live" and remote classes showed no significant differences. Students appreciated the time and money saved in not having to commute as well as the fact that if they missed a class, it was available on videotape.

Plans for expansion of the system were well under way in 1985. A third television classroom accommodating 60 students was constructed in Latrobe Hall at Homewood, a smaller classroom was being designed for the Traylor Building in East Baltimore, and teleconference rooms were planned for Homewood and APL.

During the break between academic sessions in the

Among many applications of new communications technology at Johns Hopkins is this instructional television facility at the G.W.C. Whiting School of Engineering. It is linked via interactive microwave to similar classrooms at the Medical Institutions and at the Applied Physics Laboratory.

summer of 1984, the University installed at Homewood one of the most modern telephone-data transmission systems available—an integrated voice-data digital AT&T System 85. The need for improved data handling had been apparent for some time as the use of computers in almost all fields of research proliferated. The new system provided high-speed transmission between on-campus terminals and campus computing centers or local area networks, as well as conventional voice communication and provision for such advanced features as electronic mail.

At the Applied Physics Laboratory, a system similar to and compatible with the System 85 was installed, and at the East Baltimore campus, an analysis was begun of ways to modernize communications among the medical institutions. Hopkins was a leader in these moves to bring communications within and among its campuses to the highest state of available technology, and served as a model for other educational institutions that were seeking to upgrade their facilities.

The full impact of these advances in communication was not immediately apparent, but expectations were high that the new technology would permit work in the Hopkins tradition across divisional and professional lines to proceed with greater facility than ever before. For faculty, the ready exchange of data and the potential for joint use of instrumentation could only enhance the opportunities for interdisciplinary research. For students, computer terminals as close as their own dormitory rooms afforded access to information and analytical techniques which just a few years before had been available to only the most advanced researchers.

* * *

By the mid-1980s, there was scarcely any aspect of life at the University that had not been touched by computers. They stored and sorted mountains of data necessary for high-level research. Through information retrieval, computers made it possible for scholars to have instant access to the most obscure sources. Word-processing made the writing of letter-perfect reports and documents vastly easier for professors and students alike.

In the humanities, computers performed tasks that could

not previously have been done in a lifetime, such as a detailed calligraphic analysis of an old translation of Vergil. Computers assisted engineers at Homewood and APL in ways so pervasive that it was difficult to recall how the profession functioned without them. Specialists at the School of Continuing Studies used computer technology to revolutionize teaching and rehabilitation of the handicapped. Physicians at the Hospital were aided in medical imaging and data analysis by computers, as were musicians at Peabody in the composition and performance of their music. Astrophysicists at Homewood and at the Space Telescope Science Institute could not have performed more than a tiny fraction of their fascinating work without massive computer assistance.

* * *

215

Libraries in the Hopkins system felt the computer boom in their own special ways. By the early 1980s, all six major libraries were using computer systems to catalog new acquisitions and to request or lend materials on interlibrary loan.

At Homewood, the Milton S. Eisenhower Library was consistently a pioneer in adopting electronic-age technology. At the time of its 20th anniversary in 1984, the library was in the midst of one of its biggest undertakings to date: conversion of the traditional card catalog system to a computerized catalog. It was the first large research library to do so. The computerized bibliography was eventually to be made available via computer terminals throughout the University.

Among earlier applications of the new technology by the library were a computerized literature search service, a tele-facsimile arrangement for obtaining copies of material from libraries across the country, computerized information on book availability, a microcomputer laboratory for use by members of the Hopkins community, and a Kurtzweil machine for electronic vocalization of printed material for the visually impaired. In 1985, the library received one of ten grants made by the National Endowment for the Humanities to major research libraries to enter bibliographic information on archival material into the Research Libraries Information Network, a national computer data base.

The William H. Welch Medical Library on the East Baltimore campus had also been consistently in the forefront of the application of computer technology, in the form of both new clinical information systems and computer access to its vast store of medical literature. The library offered individually tailored bibliographies via the MEDLINE network of the National Library of Medicine and several other national data bases. Also available were terminals which provided students with access to computer-assisted instruction, using the resources of the Harvard and University of Illinois medical schools. In 1985, the checkout system was automated and integrated with catalog data so that the availability of particular items could be instantly determined. Applications of similar usefulness were in place at the R.E. Gibson Library of the Applied Physics Laboratory, including several on-line national data bases in science and technology.

* * *

In June 1985, a giant step forward was taken in the University's continuing effort to make available the most advanced computer capabilities. It took the form of an agreement between Johns Hopkins and the country's second largest computer manufacturer, Digital Equipment Corporation, to develop a new computer network embracing the Baltimore campuses and the Applied Physics Laboratory that would greatly enhance productivity in research and instruction and assist in the work of the central University administration.

The agreement made available to Hopkins at a reduced rate some $15 million worth of computing and networking resources from the Digital firm, equipment far more powerful and versatile than that which the University had in place. "Hopkins is a decentralized institution," Dr. Muller said at a press conference, "both structurally and geographically, and networking technology is therefore especially important here. Through Digital we are acquiring the tools to explore the enormous potential of this technology across the spectrum of University activities and business."

In addition to five interconnected local area networks at Homewood, networks were planned for the School of Medicine, the School of Hygiene and Public Health, and APL, as well as at the Space Telescope Science Institute. "A major goal of Johns Hopkins is to create an electronically integrated campus to facilitate interdisciplinary research and the rapid exchange of information between the University's divisions," said engineering dean David VandeLinde at the time of the announcement. "The networking technology we are acquiring from Digital represents a major step in this direction."

* * *

The computer age resulted in many less momentous changes in Hopkins life, as might be expected. In October 1984, the *Johns Hopkins Magazine* reported: "That hopeless jumble of outdated messages about rides to Albany, lost kittens, and vegetarian, non-smoking housemates preferred—the college bulletin board—may soon be a thing of the past. The Electronic Bulletin Board is here, in operation, at the Homewood campus." The magazine was reporting on a computerized bank of messages in 14 categories that could be punched up by anyone using the Homewood computer system.

And what about the 1985 Homecoming lacrosse battle with Navy? Alumni groups in a dozen U.S. cities were able to see it as for the first time in lacrosse history, a college game was televised via satellite to its most ardent supporters from New York to San Francisco.

The Blue Jays obliged with a 24-10 win.

Hopkins' global outreach

The three areas of thematic importance for the future that were singled out by Dr. Muller in his centennial dinner speech—the reintegration of knowledge, the growth of continuing education, and the impact of the computer-communications revolution—were, indeed, of critical significance to Johns Hopkins in the decade that followed, as even the preceding brief survey of activities in the various University divisions illustrates.

But another concept emerged with ever-expanding strength to take its place as a fourth basic theme in the modern history of Johns Hopkins. That was the international dimension of the University, not only in the sense that its teaching and research were of "world class" quality, which had been true throughout its history, but to the extent that the spreading impact of its science and scholarship had made Johns Hopkins an increasingly recognized presence around the world.

Hopkins was an international institution from its beginnings. The genes for this trait were in the seeds of the University's founding—Hopkins was a New World variant of a European theme. Gilman, a Yale alumnus, had also studied in Berlin. His first faculty consisted of a British mathematician (Sylvester), a young American physicist who had worked in Germany with Helmholtz (Rowland), a South Carolina-born classical scholar who had studied at Princeton and Gottingen (Gildersleeve), a chemist who mastered his craft in Munich under Liebig (Remsen), a T.H. Huxley-trained biologist (Martin), and an Oxford-schooled classicist (Morris). In medicine, the first physician-in-chief (Osler) was Canadian-born and educated in Montreal, London, Leipzig,

> *'The modern research university... has come along in just the decades since World War II. And that modern research university... is really an international institution.'*
>
> Steven Muller

and Vienna. With such individuals molding the character of the University in its infancy, a strong international trait was destined to evolve.

The cycle was still reenergizing itself a century later, when the man in the office first occupied by Gilman, Steven Muller, was German-born and educated in Germany, Great Britain, and the United States.

* * *

Dr. Muller expressed his views on the growing global outreach of Johns Hopkins in a television interview in 1985, saying: "The University community has always been international, with scholars coming from different countries. What's new is that a creation called the modern research university, which does teaching but also big-time research, has come along in just the decades since World War II. And that modern research university, very different from colleges and teaching universities, is really an international institution.

"In the initial period after the war," he continued, "America had not a monopoly but such great leadership in science that American universities were almost a world unto themselves, ahead of almost everybody else. That changed, so that now very distinguished research is done on the continent of Europe, increasingly in Japan, and in other places. The modern research university is not only a national but an international institution, and the global outreach is a reflection of that."

Dr. Muller added that there was a community of only about 100 internationally recognized research universities in the modern western sense throughout the world, and that Hopkins was clearly among that group. These were institutions with individual visibility in areas in which they were acknowledged to excel on a global scale. Interaction among those institutions was close and destined to become even stronger, he predicted, aided by the revolution in communications technology and necessitated by growing highly sophisticated research interests among scientists and scholars whose language was that of a discipline and not of any one nation.

In addition to this new dimension that was identified with modern research universities, Johns Hopkins in the early

Johns Hopkins' global outreach is exemplified in the Hopkins-Nanjing Center for Chinese and American Studies, construction of which was well underway in 1985. The Center is among the first cooperative educational ventures between the United States and the People's Republic of China since resumption of diplomatic relations between the two countries.

1980s provided numerous examples of more traditional kinds of international activities and exchanges. They included:

- The Center for European Studies in Bologna, the Villa Spelman, and the Johns Hopkins-Nanjing Center for Chinese and American Studies, discussed earlier.

- The vast catalog of overseas health programs directed or supported by the School of Hygiene and Public Health, which in 1984 had more people involved in international health programs than any other university in America.

- The International Fellows Program of the Center for Metropolitan Planning and Research; in 1980, the program celebrated its tenth anniversary with a major Baltimore-Washington conference of European and American urban experts.

- JHPIEGO, an acronym for Johns Hopkins Program for International Education in Gynecology and Obstetrics, a medical education program supported by the U.S. Agency for International Development that since 1974 had upgraded the skills of thousands of physicians and health professionals in the area of reproductive biology in more than 100 developing countries.

- A program under which Hopkins residents in psychiatry could switch apartments, cars, and jobs with British counterparts and spend a year at Maudsley Hospital, a division of the University of London's Institute of Psychiatry.

- The election by the United Nations General Assembly of Stephen M. Schwebel, Edward B. Burling Professor of International Law at SAIS, as a judge of the International Court of Justice.

- A program under which the Department of Sociology trained both academic researchers and policy-making personnel of international agencies concerned with issues of development.

- The establishment in 1983 of the American Institute for Contemporary German Studies, an independently incorporated affiliate of Johns Hopkins in Washington, D.C., chaired initially by former Secretary of Defense and NATO Ambassador Donald Rumsfeld with President Muller as vice-chairman. The Institute was set up as a center for research on post-World War II German issues—politics, economics, foreign policy, society, and history of both West Germany and East Germany—with a view toward deepening understanding in the United States of post-war German problems and training a new generation of American experts on modern Germany.

* * *

Early into its second century of existence, Johns Hopkins fit the mold of an international research university by many sets of measures. Among other distinctions, its scientists and scholars had given their own or the institution's name to an elementary atomic particle, a mineral field in Africa, two glaciers in Alaska, and a crater on the moon. The last is especially pertinent in view of Hopkins' selection as host university for the Space Telescope Science Institute, which elevated the University's international dimension to an entirely new realm. Involvement in the Institute's programs, added to traditional commitments, placed Johns Hopkins in a stronger position than ever before to make a unique contribution to worldwide intellectual and scientific life in the late 20th century and beyond.

To advance knowledge—and diffuse it

In 1978, the Johns Hopkins University Press marked the 100th anniversary of its founding, an occasion highlighted by the selection of Baltimore for the annual meeting of the American Association of University Presses as well as by appropriate local celebration. As the oldest continuously operating university press in the country (Cornell started one in 1863 but closed it 15 years later), the Hopkins operation had long been recognized for the quality of its publications and for major innovations in the field of scholarly publishing.

Although respected from the beginning as a pioneer in the publication of academic journals, the Press through its first 70 years had made relatively little comparable impact in other areas of scholarly publishing. In the late 1940s, its production consisted—along with its journals—of about a dozen books a year representing a sales volume of $75,000. There was a staff of four with a "warehouse" located in World War II Quonset huts set up at the bottom of light shafts in Gilman Hall.

All this began to change with the arrival in 1948 of a new director, Harold E. Ingle. During his 26 years of service, the staff was enlarged, book production was increased, offices were secured on an entire floor of Whitehead Hall, and a large off-campus

By 1984, the Press had become one of the largest American university presses, publishing about 100 new books a year, along with 22 journals.

warehouse was acquired. Upon his retirement in 1974, Mr. Ingle was succeeded by Jack G. Goellner, who carried on the move toward broader production while maintaining high standards of professionalism.

As the evolutionary product of Gilman's conviction that one of a university's noblest duties was "to advance knowledge, and to diffuse it ... far and wide," the Press's imprint is still governed by a faculty-appointed editorial board, and its publication list reflects many of the University's main intellectual and research interests. Literary studies, history, economics, political science, and the history of science and medicine by tradition have been prominent subjects among its offerings. More recent catalogs show increased interest in psychology, the biomedical sciences and public health, natural history, and the history of technology. Since 1970, a number of books about Baltimore and Maryland that were not in the strictest sense scholarly works were also published and proved to be highly popular.

Among the publishing highlights of the Press's recent history are the 11-volume variorum edition of the works of English poet Edmund Spenser; the *Johns Hopkins Atlas of Functional Human Anatomy,* in use throughout the world; *Johns Hopkins Studies in the History of Technology; Walker's Mammals of the World;* numerous books on international economics published through a long-standing affiliation with the World Bank; *A Documentary History of the First Federal Congress;* as well as multi-volume editions of the letters and papers of such figures as Dwight D. Eisenhower, George C. Marshall, Frederick Law Olmsted, Mary Wollstonecraft Shelley, and Thomas A. Edison.

By 1984, the Press had become one of the largest American university presses, publishing about 100 new books a year, along with 22 journals. There was a staff of 75, and gross revenues for the year exceeded $5 million. Ancillary operations included a British publishing subsidiary, Johns Hopkins Press, Ltd., which published all University books in England and distributed them throughout the United Kingdom, Europe, and the Middle East. Several cooperative groups and a network of sales agents represented the Press elsewhere in the world, including Latin America and Africa. Altogether, about 20 percent of total sales were being made outside the United States. There was also a Press-operated consortium founded in 1977 that provided to other scholarly publishers such distribution services as order handling, data processing, warehousing, shipping, and billing. By 1984, there were 19 other publishers in the consortium, which was shipping nearly a million books a year.

The magnitude of the Johns Hopkins operation did not impinge on the quality of its products. In 1984 alone, the Press won 30 prizes for scholarly and graphic excellence.

Other honors in recent years included Columbia University's Bancroft Prize, the Ralph Waldo Emerson Award by Phi Beta Kappa, four Dexter Prizes from the Society for the History of Technology, and other awards from the American Academy and Institute of Arts and Letters, *Publishers Weekly*, the Medieval Academy of America, the American Historical Association, the Society of Architectural Historians, the American Institute of Industrial Engineers, and the Wildlife Society.

In 1983, the National Endowment for the Humanities awarded the Press a $250,000 challenge grant, the largest ever made to a university press. Such presses traditionally operate with little institutional support and are more concerned with staying solvent than making a profit. The NEH grant was intended to help the Press attain long-term financial stability through the creation of an endowment and a capital resources fund. Required to match the grant on a three-to-one basis, the Press embarked on the first general fund-raising campaign in its history.

Finally, and with an unavoidable touch of irony, it must be noted that the Press's best-seller in terms of profit is not a book at all, but an 18-inch-high articulated plastic model of a human skeleton, a teaching aid developed at the Medical Institutions by Leon Schlossberg and known among the Press staff as "Mr. Bones." First "published" in 1961, the skeleton by the time of the Press's centennial had sold 26,000 copies and brought in $500,000. Its success prompted the development of a companion model of the human surface anatomy, known in-house, naturally, as "Mr. Muscles."

* * *

Another front-rank publishing enterprise at the University continues to be the *Johns Hopkins Magazine,* since 1972 under the editorship of Elise Hancock. A consistent award-winner in its field, the magazine's recent honors include the nation's top writing prize for college and university periodicals—the Harper's Magazine Award for Excellence—in 1978, the 1980 Robert Sibley Magazine of the Year Award by *Newsweek* magazine, and its selection seven times as the nation's best alumni magazine by the American Alumni Council and the Council for the Advancement and Support of Education.

In 1981, the magazine initiated a unique experiment in college and university publication, a cooperative venture to enable a number of institutions to share editorial material and publishing expenses for their alumni periodicals. Known as the Alumni Magazine Consortium, the group now includes five colleges and universities besides Hopkins which share a quarterly 16-page "core" of articles of broad interest that is bound inside the publications of each school. Members share editorial and production costs but benefit from economies of scale, as the consortium staff carries out all phases of production for member magazines.

228

From the halls of Garland

In the fall of 1985, an ad hoc committee of trustees of the University and Hospital recommended changes in the governance structure of the institutions. The committee noted that the University and Hospital had functioned harmoniously and in a complementary fashion in the past, citing the beneficial effects of the joint presidency between 1972 and 1983 and the creation of the Trustee Policy Committee. However, the committee felt that in view of the increasing complexity and widening scope of the activities of the two institutions, structural changes should be made which would ensure the permanence of the existing relationship through changes in leadership which would inevitably come in time.

The committee's report stated: "The most important considerations underlying the Committee's deliberations are preservation of the affiliation of the Institutions, establishment of policy in matters of joint concern, mutually agreeable succession of leadership of the Institutions and effective management of joint projects..." As examples of recently expanded joint activities, the report cited the acquisition of Francis Scott Key Medical Center, creation of the Dome Corporation, development of the Johns Hopkins Health Plan, real estate management and financing, and acquisition of North Charles General Hospital and Wyman Park Health Systems.

The committee recommended creation of several new organizational structures which would have the effect of binding the University and Hospital more closely and permanently together.

* * *

A number of administrative changes in the years following the centennial should be noted. Richard P. Longaker, former UCLA department chairman and dean, was appointed provost of Johns Hopkins in 1976 upon the resignation of Harry Woolf, who left to become director of the Institute for Advanced Study at Princeton, N.J. In 1978, George E. Owen, dean of the Faculty of Arts and Sciences, became dean of the Homewood Faculties; he was succeeded in his former position by Sigmund R. Suskind. In 1982, Dr. Owen returned to teaching and research and was named University Professor.

In 1983, B.J. Norris, then director of public affairs for the Medical Institutions, was named vice president for communications and public affairs, the first woman to hold a vice presidency at the University. Ross Jones, a 1953 alumnus of the School of Arts and Sciences who had been vice president for public affairs, was named vice president and secretary of the University; in addition to working closely with the board of trustees, his duties included coordinating the work of a series of advisory councils which had been created to counsel the deans in each academic division on the development of programs and new resources. Also in that year, Dr. Suskind was succeeded as dean of Arts and Sciences by George W. Fisher, a 1963 Hopkins Ph.D. in geology and previously chairman of the Department of Earth and Planetary Sciences.

In 1984, Robert D.H. Harvey stepped down as chairman of the University's board of trustees after 16 years of service and was succeeded by George G. Radcliffe, a 1947 Arts and Sciences alumnus. Mr. Harvey had held the chairmanship through difficult transitional times, and his dedication was sincerely praised by President Muller. Mr. Radcliffe had served as vice chairman of the board and chairman of the Annual Fund from 1979 to 1981. Also in 1984, it was Dr. Muller's painful duty to report the death of Dr. Owen at the age of 62. One of the liveliest intellects ever to grace the Homewood campus, Dr. Owen was memorialized with the establishment of fellowships in his name for outstanding graduate students in the School of Arts and Sciences.

In 1985, Robert C. Bowie, vice president for finance and treasurer of the University since 1977, was named senior vice president for administration. Robert M. Wilson, former director of personnel programs, was named to a new vice presidency for personnel programs. Also in 1985, a new deanship for administration was established at Homewood to be responsible for academic support services, student services, and extracurricular activities. The first incumbent was Robert S. Welch, former assistant vice chancellor for student affairs at the University of Massachusetts.

* * *

"For once this letter begins on a sad note," wrote Dr. Muller in his memorandum to alumni, parents, and friends of June 20, 1985. "You will already know of the death of President Emeritus Milton S. Eisenhower on May 2, in his 85th year. None of us need to be reminded of the extraordinary leadership which Dr. Eisenhower provided to the University in his unprecedented two terms in office, from 1956 to 1967, and again in 1971 to 1972.... Because he remained in Baltimore, he was a constant, visible and cherished presence for most of us at the University. We have lost not only a former President but a close and dear friend, who retained up to the very end his abiding interest in the University, in students and in our visions of the future, as well as in the issues that confront all Americans. His life was exceptionally rich and full and long, so that sadness is leavened by enormous respect for his achievements; but he is sorely missed."

A family of 60,000

More than 60,000 men and women around the world are now counted as Johns Hopkins alumni, by virtue of either holding a University degree or having completed at least a year of full-time study as a matriculated degree candidate. The three largest clusters are in the Baltimore City-Baltimore County-Annapolis area, where more than a third (24,000) reside; the New York City area, with 6,500; and the Washington, D.C., area, with about 6,000.

Dr. Eisenhower frequently gave credit to the University's alumni for their support. Dr. Muller was no less lavish in praising the commitment demonstrated by alumni during his administration. Since the centennial and the Hopkins Hundreds campaign—in which alumni support was crucial—the number of chapters across the country has risen from 36 to 50, and the membership of the Alumni Association has doubled. About 17,500 sign up annually, paying nearly $400,000 in dues that support alumni programs and provide funds for special student and University projects.

While groups were being organized as early as the 1880s, the building of an alumni constituency began in earnest with the hiring in 1947 of Osmar P. Steinwald as first full-time director of alumni relations, as noted earlier. A member of the Class of 1928, Mr. Steinwald also ran the annual alumni fund drive. He retired in 1970 and was succeeded by Stanley E. Blumberg, B.A. 1935, under whose leadership the association grew to 48 regional U.S. chapters and six professional chapters. In addition, there were organized alumni groups in several overseas locations, including Japan and the Philippines.

Among the projects developed by Mr. Blumberg was a series of alumni foreign tours, which proved so popular that now the association arranges an average of six trips a year. Mr. Blumberg also initiated the Alumni College, a week-long summer retreat in which about 100 alumni meet with Hopkins faculty experts in an informal exploration of issues of serious intellectual concern, now in its 11th year. The Alumni Association and the Office of Alumni Relations also stage the annual Homecoming weekend each spring.

Each of the six professional chapters—APL, Evening College engineers, Hygiene and Public Health, Nursing, Peabody, and SAIS—is the focus of alumni programming conducted by the individual school or division. In addition, the School of Medicine has its own alumni organization.

Mr. Blumberg retired in 1983 and was succeeded by William J. Evitts, a member of the Class of 1964 and holder of a Hopkins Ph.D. in history. Two chapters have been added since that time, a program of special reunions for holders of graduate degrees has been inaugurated, and the number of special programs for Baltimore-area alumni has been substantially increased. The association under Dr. Evitts also arranged for televising the 1985 Homecoming lacrosse game to alumni groups across the country.

Funding for the future

On September 22, 1984, Johns Hopkins made headlines by announcing a campaign to raise $450 million for the University and Hospital over a five-year period. It was the most ambitious goal in the history of American higher education to that time. "The size of the effort is not of our own making," President Muller had told the University trustees. "It is a command performance, called for by circumstances unequaled in humanity's past. Johns Hopkins must rise to new heights, or fail the purposes for which it was created. The only escape is into mediocrity."

The overall goal of the drive, named The Campaign for Johns Hopkins, is twofold: first, to reshape the University's financial profile by increasing endowment and using the added income to reduce dependence on tuition and uncertain federal money; second, to refit Hopkins for world leadership.

A university, Dr. Muller said, "is the human institution fashioned to unlock discovery and prepare men and women in the uses of knowledge." Given the tumultuous changes being brought about by new technologies, he added, "every university confronts—and composes— the core of the problem. How well will its graduates serve?"

President Muller in early 1982 called upon the faculties and the administration to undertake an intensive self-evaluation and develop a plan to move the University into the 21st century.

The campaign was launched at a gala affair on the Homewood campus on the evening of September 22, when 1,100 guests and celebrities gathered for cocktails, dixieland jazz, a banquet, and speeches held in tents on the main quadrangles. Entertainer Steve Allen was master of ceremonies, weaving humor and warmth into a program that featured talks and testimonials by Baltimore's Mayor Schaefer, University trustee Sol M. Linowitz, 1947 alumnus and *New*

235

York Times columnist Russell Baker, and boxing champion Sugar Ray Leonard, who praised the care he received at the Wilmer Institute when a detached retina threatened his vision. There was also a spectacular audiovisual laser show. The festive mood was climaxed when campaign chairman Morris W. Offit announced that the drive was off to an impressive start with $114 million—more than the total raised by the Hopkins Hundreds campaign—already in hand in the form of advance gifts and pledges.

* * *

A campaign to raise nearly half a billion dollars does not spring to life overnight. Concerned about problems of sustaining and enriching the Hopkins tradition of training professionals in a world of dizzying technological and intellectual change, President Muller in early 1982 called upon the faculties and the administration to undertake an intensive self-evaluation and develop a plan to move the University into the 21st century. The challenge was to do this without sacrificing the institution's traditional characteristics of smallness, excellence, and independence. This planning effort, led by Dr. Longaker, produced a needs list that would have cost nearly a billion dollars to implement—clearly an unattainable figure. After 18 months of further deliberation, divisional priorities were translated into general categories of need totaling $450 million, a sum which was believed to be achievable.

The Joint Trustee Development Committee, under the direction of Robert H. Levi, monitored the planning process and recommended that the campaign be undertaken. At a special joint meeting of the University and Hospital trustees at the Greenbrier in White Sulphur Springs, West Virginia, in November 1983, the proposal was overwhelmingly approved. A steering committee was formed under the chairmanship of Mr. Offit, a 1957 alumnus, University trustee since 1973, and president of his own investment counseling firm in New York. His co-chairmen were H. Furlong Baldwin and Calman J. Zamoiski Jr. Unlike the Hopkins Hundreds, The Campaign for Johns Hopkins was launched without the assistance of outside consultants, relying instead on the efforts of the trustees, volunteers, and the 45-member professional development staff of the University.

* * *

The campaign goal was broken down as follows: $120 million for endowment; $80 million for construction and renovation; $125 million for research; $25 million for scientific instruments; and $100 million in current funding for academic programs, faculty support, and student aid.

Endowment was of special concern because it was the key to realigning the University's revenue structure. At the end of 1983, the endowment totaled $354 million, an all-time high which placed Hopkins 13th among American private institutions. But there was a striking gap after the top five institutions: Harvard, Princeton, Yale, Stanford, and Columbia. While 13th, Hopkins' endowment was only one-seventh of Harvard's $2.4 billion.

Endowment income provided 7 percent of the University's income in 1983, as it had ten years earlier. Federal support in that period, however, had dropped from 45 to 33 percent, meaning, among other things, an increased dependence on tuition to balance the budget. The desired postcampaign mix would increase the endowment income share of revenues to 15 percent, reducing tuition from 19 to 15 percent and allowing for only 30 percent in government support. The balance would come from private gifts and other sources.

The Campaign for Johns Hopkins did well in the early going. University and Hospital trustee Harvey M. Meyerhoff and his wife, Lyn, gave a remarkable leadership gift of $5 million to establish a digestive diseases center at the Hospital and the Albright Chair in the School of Arts and Sciences. In January 1985, Ryda and Robert H. Levi gave $2 million in unrestricted funds, one of the largest unrestricted contributions in the institution's history. Mr. Levi, a 1936 alumnus, became a Hospital trustee in 1958 and a University trustee in 1973. In recognition of their generosity, the west wing of Mudd Hall was dedicated as the Levi Building.

In December 1985, Mr. Offit was able to report that the campaign had passed the halfway point toward its goal, only a little over a year into the planned five-year effort. More than

$225 million in gifts or commitments had been received: $120 million from alumni and friends, $56.6 million from foundations and organizations, and $48.5 million from corporate donors.

It happens every spring

No history of Johns Hopkins would be complete without a few words about lacrosse, a sport which has aroused passion in the hearts of Hopkins students and alumni for more than a century.

Lacrosse is to Johns Hopkins what football is to Notre Dame and basketball to UCLA—with one major difference. Lacrosse at Homewood was never commercialized. The sport has never captured network television attention, a fact which undoubtedly helped preserve the game's distinct amateur flavor. It remains a game for athletes and aficionados, much as it was in 1928 and 1932 when it was represented by Johns Hopkins in the only Olympic Games in which the sport was played. And even though a growing number of colleges and universities in recent years have begun fielding lacrosse

Lacrosse, a rough-and-tumble game originated by North American Indians, found a home at Johns Hopkins, where it has been played since 1883. University teams participated in the 1928 and 1932 Olympic Games—the only years in which the sport was represented— and through 1985 had won 41 national championships. Shown is part of the 1980 championship squad.

teams and offering attractive recruitment incentives, Hopkins continues to assemble a succession of conference-leading and championship-winning squads and to contribute a disproportionate 25 percent of the members of the Lacrosse Hall of Fame, located appropriately in the Newton H. White Jr. Athletic Center.

Recitals of the Hopkins record, throat-tightening talk of tradition, and warm reminiscences were the order of the day on a blustery Saturday afternoon in mid-April 1983, when 800 former players and their families joined 5,300 fans at Homewood Field to celebrate 100 years of Hopkins lacrosse. Among them was Julian H. Marshall, Class of 1913 and, at 91, the oldest of the "Old Guard" players from the sport's first half-century. They reveled in the cheers of partisans at halftime in a clash between Hopkins and Army. Hopkins won— its 608th victory according to diligent research by the *Johns Hopkins Magazine*.

Later that year, the University's quest for its 39th national championship was thwarted by a 17-16 loss to Syracuse. Revenge came in 1984 when the Jays won the NCAA title in a 13-10 victory over Syracuse, a feat that was duplicated in 1985 when Hopkins humiliated the Orange 11-4 to capture its 41st national championship.

A HOPKINS CHRONOLOGY

1867—Johns Hopkins, a wealthy Baltimore Quaker merchant, incorporates the University and Hospital.

1873—Hopkins dies in Baltimore on December 24.

1874—Hopkins' will is probated in January and his fortune of nearly $7 million is divided between the University and Hospital which will bear his name. The boards of trustees of the two institutions meet for the first time in February to discuss how best to carry out the benefactor's requests.

1875—The University trustees purchase land on Howard Street in downtown Baltimore for the first campus. Daniel Coit Gilman is chosen as the University's first president.

1876—On February 22, Dr. Gilman is inaugurated and the University officially opens. During the summer, the first 20 Fellows are chosen out of 152 applicants. Classes begin in October under the first faculty: Basil L. Gildersleeve in Greek, H. Newell Martin in biology, Charles D. Morris in classics, Ira Remsen in chemistry, Henry A. Rowland in physics, and James J. Sylvester in mathematics. In November, Professor Sylvester founds the *American Journal of Mathematics,* the nation's first scholarly journal (although the first issue is not published until January 1878).

1877—Professor Remsen founds the *American Chemical Journal.*

1878—The Johns Hopkins University Press (now the oldest continuously operating university press in the United States) is founded in February. In June, the first candidates for the Ph.D. are presented to President Gilman—Henry C. Adams, Thomas Craig, Josiah Royce, and Ernest Sihler. Professor Remsen and his assistant, Constantine Fahlberg, discover saccharin.

1879—The first bachelor of arts degrees are awarded in June to George W. McCreary, A. Chase Palmer, and Edward H. Spieker.

1880—Professor Rowland invents the ruling engine for making diffraction gratings, which revolutionize the science of spectroscopy. Professor Gildersleeve founds the *American Journal of Philology.*

1882—The first Johns Hopkins lacrosse team is formed.

1883—The committee to establish the medical school meets for the first time and creates a medical faculty consisting of professors Remsen in chemistry, Martin in physiology, John Shaw Billings in hygiene, and (in 1884) William H. Welch in pathology. Woodrow Wilson enrolls as a graduate student in political science and history; he receives his Ph.D. in 1886 and later becomes the only United States president to hold such a degree.

1886—The first effort at organizing Johns Hopkins alumni is undertaken.

1887—The University suffers its first financial setback as Baltimore & Ohio Railroad stock fails. Tuition is raised and salaries are frozen.

1889—The Johns Hopkins Hospital, one of the nation's first teaching hospitals, opens in May with "The Four Doctors" at the helm—Dr. Welch, William Halsted, Howard Kelly, and William Osler. Dr. Halsted invents the rubber surgical glove. In October, the School of Nursing opens with 19 students under the direction of Isabel Hampton.

1891—The first Johns Hopkins nurses received their diplomas in June.

1892—The Women's Medical Fund reaches its goal of $500,000 to endow the School of Medicine; of this sum, Mary Elizabeth Garrett contributes $354,764. Trustees accept the conditions of the gift that women be admitted on the same terms as men and that the School maintain the highest academic standards, a major factor in Hopkins' role in changing the course of medical education in the United States.

1893—The Johns Hopkins Medical School (it was not known as the School of Medicine until 1924) opens in October with 18 students, including three women, and a faculty of 15. Dr. Welch is the first dean.

1894—The Medical School's first building, the Women's Fund Memorial Building, later known as the Anatomy Building, is completed.

1895—The Johns Hopkins chapter of Phi Beta Kappa is founded with Dr. Gilman as first president.

1897—The first physicians graduate in June from the Medical School; 14 men and one woman.

1898—The elective system, a major change in medical

education, is introduced at the Medical School.

1899—The Johns Hopkins Club is organized. It opens the following year at 706 St. Paul Street.

1901—After 25 years of service, President Gilman retires. Ira Remsen is elected to succeed him.

1902—On February 22, Dr. Remsen is inaugurated as the University's second president. Negotiations to acquire the Homewood campus are completed.

1905—The Hunterian Laboratory is completed at the Medical School.

1909—The University awards its first M.A. degree.

1911—The first summer session is held.

1912—The State of Maryland appropriates $600,000 plus $50,000 a year to found the School of Engineering. The first students are admitted in October.

1914—Frank Johnson Goodnow becomes the third president of the University.

1915—Gilman Hall, the first major building completed on the Homewood campus, is dedicated in May, along with Maryland Hall. Ground is broken for Latrobe Hall in October.

1916—The first unit of the Reserve Officers' Training Corps in the nation is established at Hopkins.

1918—The School of Hygiene and Public Health, the first of its kind in the country, opens under the direction of Dr. Welch.

1922—Elmer V. McCollum at the School of Hygiene and Public Health discovers vitamin D, following on his earlier discovery of vitamin A. At Homewood, construction of the first dormitory begins.

1923—The Pathology Building is completed at the Medical School.

1924—Remsen Hall, housing lecture halls and facilities for chemistry, opens at Homewood.

1925—President Goodnow announces a plan calling for the phasing out of all undergraduate work at the University; it is approved by the trustees the following year but abolished in 1930. In East Baltimore, the building for the School of Hygiene and Public Health opens.

1928—Two new medical buildings, the Wilmer Clinic and the Welch Medical Library, are completed.

1929—President Goodnow resigns and on July 1, Joseph Sweetman Ames becomes fourth president of the University. Levering Hall (a student center) and Rowland Hall (the physics building) are completed at Homewood. In East Baltimore, the Physiology Building is completed.

1935—Dr. Ames retires and is succeeded on July 1 as president by Isaiah Bowman.

1937—A building for the Johns Hopkins Club, a gift of the Marburg family, is completed at Homewood.

1941—Mergenthaler Hall, housing the Department of Biology, is opened at Homewood.

1942—The University assumes responsibility for the Applied Physics Laboratory in Silver Spring, Maryland, a facility established to develop the radio proximity fuze in the early days of World War II.

1944—Drs. Alfred Blalock and Helen Taussig perform the first "blue baby" operation and launch a new era in cardiac surgery.

1945—The Applied Physics Laboratory develops the first supersonic ramjet engine.

1946—The first photographs of the earth from space are produced by the Applied Physics Laboratory.

1947—All part-time courses offered by the University are consolidated into a new division, McCoy College. Using techniques developed by William B. Kouwenhoven, professor of electrical engineering, physicians at the Hospital successfully resuscitate a patient with a fibrillating heart.

1948—The Chesapeake Bay Institute is founded to study the ecology of the bay. Johns Hopkins produces the first weekly network television series affiliated with a university, *The Johns Hopkins Science Review.*

1949—Detlev W. Bronk becomes the University's sixth president in January. The Department of Biophysics is endowed by Mrs. Thomas Jenkins, and construction of a building to house it is begun at Homewood.

1950—The University assumes responsibility for the School of Advanced International Studies in Washington, which was established in 1943 by the Foreign Service Educational Foundation.

1953—President Bronk resigns to head the Rockefeller

Institute. Lowell J. Reed succeeds him as the University's seventh president.

1954—Three new buildings are completed at Homewood: Shriver Hall, providing a large auditorium; Ames Hall, with facilities for psychology and engineering departments; and a second dormitory.

1955—The School of Advanced International Studies establishes a center in Bologna, Italy, the first American graduate school for the study of international relations in Europe.

1956—President Reed resigns and the trustees elect Milton S. Eisenhower as his successor.

1957—Dr. Eisenhower is inaugurated as the University's eighth president on Commemoration Day, February 22. The Washington Center of Foreign Policy Research is established at the School of Advanced International Studies. A Master of Arts in Teaching program is developed at Homewood. The Applied Physics Laboratory announces discovery of the Doppler satellite tracking system.

1958—The curriculum of the School of Medicine is revised to accelerate the pace of medical education, increase the scientific content, and stress relationships between medicine and the humanities and science. Reed Hall, a residence building for the School of Medicine, is opened. Space research and development is accelerated at the Applied Physics Laboratory.

1959—The new $5 million Wood Basic Science Building opens at the School of Medicine. A Department of Social Relations is established at Homewood.

1960—A $6 million grant, largest general purpose grant in University history, is received from the Ford Foundation. A $4.2 million campaign is launched for improvements at the School of Advanced International Studies.

1961—A new chair is endowed which in 1964 evolves into the Department of the History of Science. The School of Engineering becomes the School of Engineering Science, and a new Department of Mechanics embraces the disciplines of civil, mechanical, and aeronautical engineering. The Department of International Health is established at the School of Hygiene and Public Health.

1962—Barton Hall, a new home for Electrical Engineering,

and the Carnegie Embryological Laboratory open at Homewood. A Department of Statistics is established in the School of Arts and Sciences.

1963—The Evening College introduces the Master of Liberal Arts program. The Biophysics Building opens at the School of Medicine.

1964—A new $4.7 million library at Homewood opens and is later named for Dr. Eisenhower; Macaulay Hall is completed. Construction is completed in East Baltimore on the Children's Medical and Surgical Center, Wilmer Institute research wing, and radiological science wing of the School of Hygiene and Public Health. An affiliation is established between the School of Medicine and the Kennedy Institute. The School of Advanced International Studies occupies a new building on Massachusetts Avenue in Washington.

1965—The Newton H. White Jr. Athletic Center and a new classroom building, later named for G. Wilson Shaffer, are completed at Homewood.

1966—The Humanities Center is established at Homewood to coordinate interdisciplinary humanistic studies at undergraduate through postdoctoral levels. The Faculty of Philosophy and the Faculty of Engineering merge into a single Faculty of Arts and Sciences. Dunning Hall is completed at Homewood. The Center for Research in the Social Organization of Schools is established. McCoy College is renamed the Evening College.

1967—Dr. Eisenhower retires on June 30. Lincoln Gordon is chosen as his successor.

1968—On February 22, Dr. Gordon is inaugurated as the University's ninth president. The Turner Auditorium and the Traylor Research Laboratory open at the School of Medicine, and the Stebbins wing of the School of Hygiene and Public Health is completed. The Center for Urban Affairs, later known as the Center for Metropolitan Planning and Research, is founded.

1969—In October, the Academic Council votes to admit female undergraduates starting in the 1970-1971 school year; in November, the trustees make the decision official. The Steinwald Alumni House opens on North Charles Street across from the Homewood campus.

1970—Student concern over national policy in the Vietnam War, military recruiting on campus, the governance of the University, and other issues culminates in a two-day student strike at Homewood in April. The first 90 female undergraduates enroll in September.

1971—High inflation and a sharp downturn in federal support contribute to the gravest financial crisis in the University's history, as a budget deficit of $4.2 million is incurred for the year. In March, Dr. Gordon resigns and Dr. Eisenhower agrees to return to office on an interim basis. The first recent graduates are appointed to the University's board of trustees. Garland Hall, a new central administration building, is completed at Homewood. A new School of Health Services is created to train allied health professionals as well as nurses.

1972—Steven Muller is elected tenth president of Johns Hopkins and inaugurated on Commemoration Day in February. The departments of statistics, computer science, and operations research are merged into a Department of Mathematical Sciences at Homewood. A return to financial stability is begun as budget deficits are sharply cut.

1973—Dr. Muller announces the Hopkins Hundreds campaign to raise $100 million by 1976, the University's centennial year. In February, the trustees approve the first balanced budget in several years. The Evening College opens off-campus centers in Columbia, Maryland, and at Goucher College in Towson. The Applied Physics Laboratory develops a revolutionary rechargeable heart pacemaker. The first students enroll in the School of Health Services.

1974—The Hopkins Hundreds campaign reaches the halfway point toward its goal. A new Hopkins Union adjoining Levering Hall is opened. In East Baltimore, ground is broken for a new complex of buildings, including a cancer center and teaching and patient facilities.

1975—In April, the trustees adopt the third balanced budget in a row. The Evening College inaugurates its first doctoral program, an Ed.D. in human communications disorders. Ceremonies in September launch the University's centennial celebration; initial results of the Hopkins Hundreds campaign make possible the creation of 20 new professorial chairs and substantially buttress the endowment.

1976—The University marks its 100th anniversary with an array of scholarly symposia celebrating a century of Johns Hopkins contributions to science and scholarship, and with a special Centennial Commemoration Day Convocation on February 22. In May, Hopkins Hundreds chairman Alonzo G. Decker Jr. announces that the campaign has exceeded its goal and raised $109 million. Homewood House is dedicated as a National Historic Landmark. German Chancellor Helmut Schmidt addresses a special Bicentennial Convocation in July. The National Aeronautics and Space Administration selects the Applied Physics Laboratory to build spacecraft instruments for a planned voyage to the outer planets.

1977—Johns Hopkins announces an affiliation with Baltimore's Peabody Institute, a leading but financially troubled school of music, adding a new cultural dimension to the scope of University activities. The new Hopkins Comprehensive Cancer Center is dedicated in April. The first class of baccalaureate nursing students graduate at the School of Health Services. The School of Advanced International Studies establishes a Center of Brazilian Studies, the first of its kind in the United States.

1978—Drs. Daniel Nathans and Hamilton O. Smith, of the Department of Microbiology, share the 1978 Nobel Prize for Medicine with a Swiss researcher for their contributions to the discovery of restriction enzymes, which opens the door to the new field of genetic engineering. A lack of financial support and changing conditions in the health care delivery field force the closing of the School of Health Services; planning begins to honor the University's commitment to nursing education. The Johns Hopkins University Press marks its centennial year.

1979—A new School of Engineering is established at Homewood upon the recommendation of a special committee and the receipt of $5 million in new endowment for the school; named for G.W.C. Whiting, the school opens in September. The first of three stages in construction of a new biology building at Homewood is completed and dedicated as Seeley G. Mudd Hall. In a time of national decline in the college-age population and falling SAT scores, a record 3,635 apply for the fall freshman class; 585 with SAT scores far above the national average are accepted.

1980—Peabody Institute launches a $12 million campaign to bolster its endowment, while the State of Maryland awards an unprecedented $900,000-a-year grant for three years. The University realizes a total of $21.4 million from the sale of its John Work Garrett coin collection; the funds are added to the endowment. A new Department of Neuroscience is established at the School of Medicine in response to explosive growth in the field. The School of Advanced International Studies opens a new Foreign Policy Institute.

1981—Johns Hopkins is chosen as the site for NASA's Space Telescope Science Institute, expected to be a focal point for world astronomy for decades to come. The Chesapeake Bay Institute occupies new quarters at Shady Side, Maryland, a gift from Gould, Inc. Renovation of Homewood Field is completed. In East Baltimore, the new Preclinical Teaching Building of the School of Medicine is opened.

1982—At Homewood, Olin Hall is dedicated in February. A unique center for Chinese and American studies is announced in cooperation with the University of Nanjing in the People's Republic of China. Trustees approve a $24 million Student Amenities Program to finance new and renovated dormitory space and food service facilities at Homewood. The School of Medicine and Hospital mark the completion of a ten-year, $150 million modernization program with the dedication of three major new buildings, including a $42 million center for neurological diseases. The School of Hygiene and Public Health inaugurates a new program in environmental health. The 250,000-volume Peabody Library Collection becomes a part of the University. A new U.S.-Japan Study Center opens at the School of Advanced International Studies.

1983—Trustees approve the establishment of a new School of Nursing as a cooperative venture of the University and three Baltimore hospitals. In Arts and Sciences, the departments of English, History, and History of Art are ranked among the nation's top ten. Construction of Mudd Hall is completed at Homewood. The School of Medicine develops a new program—FlexMed—to reverse a trend toward excessive goal-oriented training among premedical students. Peabody's renovated concert hall opens in October. The Homewood and East Baltimore campuses and the Applied Physics Laboratory are joined by a microwave communications link, and plans are developed for televising classes between Homewood and APL.

1984—The Campaign for Johns Hopkins, an effort to raise $450 million for the University and Hospital, is announced; it is the largest campaign in the history of American higher education to date. The Evening College changes its name to the School of Continuing Studies. In East Baltimore, the Clayton Heart Center is dedicated. Baltimore City Hospitals becomes a part of the Johns Hopkins Medical Institutions and is renamed Francis Scott Key Medical Center. Physicist Samuel T. Durrance is chosen by NASA for a Space Shuttle flight to carry HUT, a Hopkins-built ultraviolet telescope, into space. The Department of Environmental Health Sciences at the School of Hygiene and Public Health is ranked as the largest of its kind in the world. The new School of Nursing opens with a class of 30 students.

1985—A Center for Astrophysical Sciences is established by the School of Arts and Sciences, an outgrowth of Hopkins' increasing eminence in this field. The National Institute on Aging selects Hopkins as the site for a major research center on Alzheimer's disease. The School of Medicine drops the traditional Medical College Admissions Test as a requirement for applicants in order to encourage broader premedical education. The University enters a cooperative venture with Montgomery County, Maryland, to establish a graduate education facility in the county. Hopkins successfully closes a $180 million tax-exempt bond issue to help finance new construction and renovation throughout the institution. The Peabody affiliation is made permanent. The Campaign for Johns Hopkins passes the halfway mark 15 months after its launching, with more than $225 million raised.

BIBLIOGRAPHY

A History of the University Founded by Johns Hopkins;
   John C. French.
Pioneer: A History of the Johns Hopkins University;
   Hugh Hawkins.
*The Johns Hopkins Hospital and the Johns Hopkins School of
   Medicine;* Alan M. Chesney.
Heritage of Excellence; Thomas B. Turner.
It Happened at Hopkins; Augusta Tucker.
Daniel Coit Gilman and the Protean Ph.D.;
   Francesco Cordasco.
*Daniel Coit Gilman: Creator of the American Type of
   University;* Abraham Flexner.
The Life of Daniel Coit Gilman; Fabian Franklin, et al.
Johns Hopkins: A Silhouette; Helen Hopkins Thom.
*Adventures in Medical Research: A Century of Discovery at
   Johns Hopkins;* A. McGehee Harvey.
The Pioneer Century: 1876-1976; Richard Macksey.

251